MW01171302

SUPERPOWER STORYTELLING

A TACTICAL GUIDE TO TELLING THE STORIES YOU NEED TO LEAD, SELL AND INSPIRE

STEPHEN STEERS

Copyright © 2023 Stephen Peter Anderson

All rights Reserved

ISBN-9798859435272

Published 2023

AI was not used to write this book. AI was used however to standardize the format and citation of the source materials because that's terribly boring work and I'd rather write instead. You get it.

All brands, logos, product names and trademarks are the property of their respective owners.

Dedication

*To Mom and Dad for instilling me with character,
ambition and curiosity in all things.*

To Marc for teaching me what brotherhood truly is.

And to you, the reader.

*Stories write the world, this book is dedicated to you
for creating and sharing yours.
The world needs it.*

Table of Contents

Get your copy of the *Superpower Storytelling Workbook* here:

Scan the QR Code with your phone!

Introduction

I grew up in Queens, New York, in the 1990s. New York City was a messy place back then: It was the crack era, the city was just 15 years from the verge of bankruptcy, and homicides were at an all-time high.

As immigrants from Jamaica, West Indies, my parents worked hard and sacrificed a lot for their boys. While things outside were rough, we had an incredible childhood. A backyard with a swing set, a basketball hoop and love in our home.

However, to my dismay, my brothers and I we were not allowed to watch television during the school week. So once the sun went down and it was time to go back inside we had to find other ways to occupy minds. For entertainment, our parents told us to read books, play our instruments, make origami or listen to cassette tapes from the *Golden Age of Radio.*

I opted for the latter. It changed everything.

The *Golden Age of Radio* was an era of pre-television radio entertainment from the 1930s- 1950s. The shows crossed many genres. Showcasing stories about hard-boiled detectives, Westerns, comedies, horror, etc.

I LOVED to listen to those stories. The shows conjured up lush scenes of vibrant color, painful heartbreak and suspense in my young mind.

Some of my favorite shows that I still listen to as an adult include: *The Adventures Sam Spade, Pat Novak for Hire, Gunsmoke, Hopalong Cassidy, Have Gun Will Travel, Nero Wolfe, Richard Diamond, The Adventures of Rocky Jordan, The Marx Brothers, The Green Hornet* and *The Whistler,* to name a few.

Building skis with K'nex before school, circa 1994

It blew my mind as a child when I learned the ingredients of these radio broadcasts. I couldn't believe that the stories weren't actually happening while I listened to them and were simply actors who sat in a room, reading scripts into a microphone and a foley artist creating the soundscape.

I would wake up with the first rays of sunlight and hasten to my sets of Legos and K'nex put on a cassette tape and start building while I listened to stories. I would build items with no instruction manual, flowing and letting my inspiration take me where it dared. My parents would have to pry me away from the Lego and K'nex sets to eat breakfast and leave in time to make it to school.

As soon as I got home from school, I raced to my room to pick up where I left off. A radio show cassette in the boombox, Legos in my hand and my imagination running wild.

Those were great memories and I'm grateful my parents encouraging me to dive deeper into that side of my mind.

These are the moments that spawned my love of storytelling. It all started with creating characters to exist in my Lego and K'nex universe. I'd craft follow-up stories about characters from the Radio Shows. I'd define their struggles and take pride in their progress. I felt like I knew these fictional characters even though they were created decades before I was born.

And as I got older, all the stories I listened to, helped me see patterns in human psychology. I've learned that while some of the details of human interaction change over time, humans still want the same things: better health, more wealth and stronger relationships. Furthermore, I learned that humans will go to great lengths to achieve them.

I became clear to me that the storyteller has a major influence on the actions we take and decisions we make.

How you ask?

To answer this question, let's talk about one of my favorite quotes. It traces back to a Greek poet-philosopher from the era of Caesar Augustus, called Quintus Horatius Flaccus, known to us in English as Horace. Horace once wrote:

> *"Change but the name, and you are the subject of the story."*

I love this quote because it's true! Think about some of your favorite stories from film, television or in your business. You've more than likely thought of yourself as having the ability to achieve similar results or surmount similar obstacles.

Stories paint pictures in the minds of listeners. They share important information, legacies and drive the masses to action.

Stories are the fabric that keep us together. Whether building a brand, selling goods and services, kicking back with your family or playing with Legos and K'nex.

Each of us – whether we know it or not – has a powerful story. Knowing how to unpack that story and share it is one of the key ways we show our uniqueness. Uniqueness and authentically cut through the noise.

Who you are is the most interesting thing about what you do. And what's at stake is the most interesting thing about why you do what you do. Combined in the form of storytelling, these premises can make you the most interesting person in the room.

In the following chapters, you'll learn frameworks to create dynamic workshops, keynotes and sales presentations, as well as practical techniques to win in casual conversation, how to smash sales objections and uncover how to leverage storytelling to be your most authentic self. You'll also learn how to use these techniques to build and scale a business or team and to achieve the greatness you seek.

Here's what this book isn't: This book isn't for the casual storyteller. This book will not make you the next Steve Jobs. I didn't write it so you could simply get a picture of what storytelling is about and how it works. It's not about sharing information on storytelling. It's about making storytelling part of your process, part of your brand and part of your business DNA. It's for those that want to make storytelling a part of their lives and to conjure deep emotional connections, no matter who is listening, reading or buying.

If you want to captivate people at the bar, sure the techniques will work. Yet, if that's the only place you want to use them, it's like driving a top-of-the-line sports car but sitting in traffic. Sure you look great but you're not using your full potential.

Lastly, this book isn't a be-all, end-all guide to storytelling. The techniques shared in these pages come from years of experience but there's always more to learn. If you want to hone storytelling and make it a real superpower, make sure to keep digging and to keep learning. Storytelling is a lifestyle.

This book is for business owners, executives and sales professionals. And those that want to go deep into human connection using story.

Please note that I use the terms "Prospects" and "Audience" synonymously in this book. Prospects are whoever you're trying to influence to make some kind of decision. This includes purchasing goods and services, accessing company budgets, raising money, creating buy-in for projects or initiatives, etc.

The goal is to get you prepared to leverage storytelling across contexts.

Why should you trust that I can help you on this journey?

It's simple. They don't teach you sales in school. They don't teach you how to be confident. They don't teach you how to be out in the world and how to make a way for yourself. So that's what I'm here for.

I love to see the lights go on in my clients' eyes when they realize they can do this. They can change their lives. They can turn their unique vision into lasting financial success.

I've consulted, advised and led workshops for more than 700 companies from 30 countries (including Google, Nike and HEC Paris Business School). I've helped clients generate millions of dollars in revenue. And I've learned that, sure, the skills I teach bring financial success. But they can also have a positive impact on every other aspect of your life.

So, I'm here to change the game. I'm here to make sales compelling, interesting and even fun. And I'm here to give you the confidence you need to win.

Forget everything you think you know about sales and leadership. Effective sales and leadership are about listening, learning and connecting through stories. Stories close the sale, never the conversation.

Are you ready to make storytelling your newest superpower?

Then keep reading.

– Stephen

P.S.

I can advise your business but I can't mind your business. So if the techniques here work for you then apply... If not, let 'em fly.

P.P.S.

Head over to Amazon and give this book a review! I'd massively appreciate it!

Scan the QR Code with your phone!

P.P.P.S

If you find any spelling errors, or mistakes in this book, email me at stephen@stephensteers.com with the page and location for a reward. I'm serious.

* * * * *

Let's start with how helping someone else tell their own story better is essential to growing your business.

CHAPTER 1

Why Your Business Needs Storytelling

Why communication of your ideas is essential to growing your business and crushing the competition

Imagine that today is one of the most beautiful days in a long time. The weather is gorgeous, not too hot, not too cold.

There's that snap in the air. It's spring, it's beautiful. And it's a Saturday. You got to sleep in and now you get the chance to spend the day with your favorite companion.

Think of your spouse, child, best friend or your pet. You suggest a brisk walk to the town square to have a nice cup of coffee. You put on that favorite jacket and you make your way down to the coffee shop.

You and your companion get in line, order your favorite caffeinated beverage then sit down to wait. You're lucky. You found the last open table right outside.

As you walk back to the table, you look over and about 50 feet (15 meters) away, you notice a blind man sitting down in the town square begging for change. Holding a sign that says: "I'm blind. Please help me."

You hasten to sit with your companion, excited for their company and the beverage that is coming. The smell of roasting beans has your palate piqued.

A few minutes pass and finally the barista calls your name. You jump up excitedly and you walk to get your beverage(s). As you walk back to your table, you see something strange.

A woman appears in the square. She's kind of out of place. She's dressed in all black, has on bright red heels, a thick woolen scarf and is carrying a large black bag.

Holding your coffee cup(s), you take special note of her presence as she stops in front of the blind man. Curiously, she opens her purse and pulls out a marker. Bending down she takes the blind man's sign and scribbles something on it.

You shake your head bewildered, as your palate anticipates the first sip of your coffee. You place the cup(s) on the table. You take the much anticipated first sip. Your beverage is superb and sparks a delightful conversation with your companion.

Taking the last sip from your coffee cup, you rise to leave. You look over at the blind man once again and notice a crowd of people surrounding him.

You can see everyone's dropping change into his coffers. Now you're even more curious. You've never seen something like this. You decide to make your way over and see what all the fuss is about.

As you walk over, you see more and more people putting more and more change in the blind man's cup. He's actually emptied the change into his jacket because the crowd filled his cup.

Your gait speeds up as you approach, pulling your companion along. All you can think as you approach is: What the heck does this sign say? You're 30 meters away. Now you're 20 meters away, the brisk spring weather heightening the effects of the caffeine.

As you look over the top of the gathered crowd with your companion, you see the new sign. Your wallet is out before you even realize. You finally reach the blind man. Placing a bill in his cup, you bid him good day. You pull your companion to your side, take in a deep breath of the brisk spring air and walk through the town square grateful.

What does the sign say? It says: "It's a beautiful day, and I can't see it."

Why this story? Well let's have a look. I want to you to think of you your brand and your business as the strange mysterious woman dressed in black with the red heels, woolen scarf and carrying the black bag.

I want you to think of your audience or prospects as the blind man. You can see things that your audience can't see and you can help them get them get the results they want. Why? Because you know how to help them tell their stories better.

Stories are key to introducing new concepts by using information and ideas that your audience or prospect already knows.

Let's talk for a second about an article of clothing that you're currently wearing. Did you try on that article of clothing in front of a mirror before you wore it out on the street? Have you ever decided against wearing something that you tried on because it didn't fit well?

That T-shirt, or those pajamas – if you're working from home – or maybe you're commuting to work and listening/reading this in a pair of jeans or a choice pair of shoes. Did you try on those items in the mirror before you wore them out of the house?

Did you check that they fit okay, if the colors looked good on you and if they paired well with some of the items you already own? Or did you ask friends or family what they thought about your new item?

I'm going to guess that you did at least one of the above before walking outside. Now you might not be a fashionista but you probably tried on the shirt before you went outside. You tried on the clothing because you liked the brand and it resonated with you. Trying on a new article of clothing is exactly how we can think about storytelling.

Let's take the concept a level further and talk about the spaghetti sauce market in USA. I know it sounds crazy but walk with me for a bit.

One of my all-time favorite authors, Malcolm Gladwell in his book *What The Dog Saw: And Other Adventures*, recounted the story of Howard Moskowitz. Moskowitz is an American market researcher best known his work on horizontal segmentation. What the heck is horizontal segmentation and what does that have to do with spaghetti sauce and storytelling?

Well, let's discuss that.

In the 1980s, Prego, a well-known spaghetti sauce manufacturer, hired Moskowitz to find out which spaghetti sauce they should make more of. During his research Moskowitz had a eureka moment.

While compiling taste test data for American consumer preferences for spaghetti sauces, he could find no clear discernible preference for one single type of spaghetti sauce. There was no "perfect" sauce for everyone. The research showed that American preferences fit into three separate camps:

> *There are people who like their spaghetti sauce plain; there are people who like their spaghetti sauce spicy; and there are people who like it extra chunky.*[11]

While on its face this may seem inconclusive, Moskowitz recognized this as an opportunity for Prego. For starters, there was no extra chunky spaghetti sauce in the 1980s. With his market data in tow, Moskowitz recommended that Prego create a new category and introduce a product line of extra chunky spaghetti sauces. "Over the next ten years, Prego turned their line of extra-chunky spaghetti sauces into 600 million dollars."

A market for chunky sauces was certainly alive and well and, as of 2004, Ragu, a key competitor to Prego, introduced 36 different varieties of spaghetti sauce to compete and serve the varied preferences of the spaghetti sauce market.

What's the lesson?

Different people have different wants. There is no one perfect solution – or perfect spaghetti sauce. There are only perfect solutions and perfect spaghetti sauces. By appealing to the varied preferences of spaghetti sauce lovers, Prego was able to satisfy their customer base with the perfect solution for them as individuals. They invited those with whom the product resonated to partake in their preference and pointed those who didn't resonate toward other products that better suited their individual preferences.

As such, each person has their own clear product or solution preference that resonates with their own specific context to tell their own story.

Stories allow us to try on new concepts, to test new products and to see new visions before we actually execute on them. Stories are the connective tissue between humans, allowing us to create human moments that resonate.

Stories allow us to bridge the gap between the humanity that we want to present and the businesses we want to scale. When you're speaking to a prospect – whether from a stage, on the phone or in person – they might not know about you or what you do.

To understand a little bit more about your methodology, the method behind the madness of your products and services, they need to meet you before anything else, and the first and best way is by telling a story.

After all, who you are is the most interesting thing about what you do, not the other way around.

Remember that every time you're about to speak with a prospect. You first have to think: "How can I help someone try on our methodology, our mindset, our expertise or get a taste of our brand experience – just like trying on a T-shirt while looking in the mirror, or picking a spaghetti sauce?" Let's create the space for our prospects to see if we fit their preferences.

If the T-shirt fits, is comfortable and matches with their current wardrobe, they'll know that it's a good option for them. If the spaghetti sauce excites their palate, they're going to buy more of it. A story is a way for folks to know that they are on the same team as you and that you're cut from the same cloth.

Stories are how people try on new concepts and experience new situations before they invest. The right stories fit like a bespoke pair of shoes, a custom-made suit or complement the palate like the perfect spaghetti sauce. Stories that aren't for us don't resonate – or fit.

Now pretend that you are wearing a fine custom-made suit. A beautiful T-shirt, a nice pair of earrings or a great pair of shoes (Nike Air Jordan's perhaps?) and folks on the street compliment you on your items, telling you that it looks really nice on you.

Can you remember when you wore your best pair of shoes and received lots of compliments? Compliments in this case are conversions. You look good, you feel good. Like making a successful sale, the story you tell about yourself through your wardrobe converted with your audience.

Stories convert.

* * * * *

You've helped people get over the hump, get comfortable with what's on offer and now they can see themselves in the action. You've changed the name and made the story about them. Remember this quote?

Change but the name and you are the subject of the story.

– Horace

Central Park

Let's pretend that we're discussing New York City – my hometown – and we're focused on Central Park. During our discussion, it comes out that you've never visited New York City.

And now you're curious about New York City. You're specifically asking me about Central Park. So I do my best to explain to you what Central Park is like.

Most people would say something like:

> "Central Park is a large park in the middle of a sprawling metropolis. It's one of the few places with trees in New York City. Some of the world's most expensive real estate surrounds the park. The Park runs from 59th street up into 120th street in Harlem. But Prospect Park in Brooklyn is way better."

Now with that explanation you might have a decent idea of what to expect from Central Park when you go. Yet, if you've never been, that explanation doesn't land as well as it could.

However, If instead our conversation went like this:

- *"Hey, have you been to Central Park?"*

- *"No. I haven't yet! I've always wanted to go! What's it like?"*

The best move would be to say:

- *"Tell me about the largest park in your hometown or where you currently live."*

And then I'd ask you questions about your local park like: "Where is it located? How large is the park? Does it run north to south? What are some of the attractions at this park? How many people visit on a weekly or yearly basis?"

You'd tell me that your local park is four square miles. It has a freshwater lake with a few smallmouth bass. You'd tell me that you enjoyed sitting by the lake and having picnics with your family when you were a child.

You'd mention that the park sits on the east end of town in one of the nicer neighborhoods. You'd tell me that you'd often go there to watch birds and of the many incredible sunrises you've watched while fishing. You'd say that next to the lake there's a basketball court and baseball diamond. And that you remember watching your first concert there as child.

I'd thank you for this information, then ask If I could share details of Central Park in comparison. I'd proceed to explain that Central Park.

New York's Central Park was the first urban landscaped park in the United States. Built in the 1850's, Central Park runs 2.5 miles (4.0 km) from north to south. Central Park sits at the center of Manhattan, connecting six historic neighborhoods (Upper East Side, Upper West Side, Lenox Hill, Lincoln Square, East Harlem and Central Harlem).

Central Park has a zoo. Compared to your small pond, where you can go fishing, we have three lakes where you can get in one of those swan boats with a date and spin around with the paddles.

Where your park has three entrances, Central Park has like 20 entrances. You can cross from the east side of Manhattan to the west through one of its three crosstown streets. They're the definition of crosstown traffic.

So much so, that Jimi Hendrix, The Voodoo Chile himself, wrote a song about it in the 1960's. Jimi Hendrix. In case you're wondering... Nope. The traffic hasn't changed since then. Not a bit. Still sucks.

There's an Egyptian obelisk in the park. You know where else has Egyptian obelisks? Egypt! Oh! We've got sports too. Baseball, basketball, ice skating and hockey, if that's your bag. It's a big park compared to the one in your hometown.

There are plenty of beautiful scenic walks you'd recognize from plenty of films...

What did I just do?

I've framed a new concept in reference to something you already know. Now I've got your attention. You're invested emotionally. It's almost like you've been there already. You're picturing yourself there.

The memories of going to your local park with your friends or your family are at the top of your mind. I brought you back to a moment of your own. This is the superpower of storytelling: helping someone to tell their own story better.

Branding

The most common objection I hear about storytelling is some version of:

> *"Telling my stories won't work with my audience. I don't want to build a brand. I don't wanna be at the face of my company. I'm not self-important."*

I understand the concern. You're not being yourself, so you're not important to your market. But that perspective is misplaced at best. Allow me to explain why. For those reading and thinking the same thing... this is the wrong way to think about yourself.

It's also the wrong way to think about your audience. This line of thinking is exactly the opposite of what your audience wants from you and your brand.

The common belief about branding is to become well known. Famous even. Everyone from every place knows your name. There's nothing wrong with being well known, but it's a different challenge entirely.

Branding for our purposes sits in direct contrast. We want to leverage storytelling to become known well. Being known well means that you've built a reputation. And you can use it in more ways that you think.

Take The Bad Guy, Chael Sonnen, a Ultimate Fighting Championship (UFC) legend, for example.

Sonnen is the first of his kind. Revered by many as the greatest trash talker In the history of sports. His often witty and cutting remarks had no equal save for the weight of his fists.

Over a career spanning two decades, Sonnen achieved success by leveraging something unique. He built his brand story to create chaos, dislike and court controversy.

Over his career he fought 49 times, earning a record of 31 and 17, achieving career winnings in the neighborhood of $1.7M which he was able to parlay into endorsements and business ventures getting him to an estimated net worth of $10 million at the time of this writing.[23] Not bad for taking a heap of punches, huh?

Why would he do this? Simple. It was his marketing tool. The persona served to drive interest to his sport and to promote his bouts.

Sonnen didn't always know this.

Sonnen stared his wrestling career at the age of nine. Long before the bad guy was born, a young Chael recalls watching boxing in the living room with his father.[4]

Together they would watch the greats of that era: Sugar Ray Leonard, Mike Tyson and Muhammad Ali.

Sitting around they would talk about the fighters they we wanted to see. They didn't want to see the guy with the good cross or the powerful jab. They wanted to watch a guy that could entertain. A guy that could tell a story that would bring them along a journey.

Sonnen points to honing his ability to captivate through story starting as early as the third grade.

> "I remember being in in the third grade and Mrs. Stanford [telling] our whole classroom to tell a story you have to have five W's: who, what, when, why. and [I] noticed that a lot of guys don't know the five W's when they tell a story."

It donned on Sonnen that a great fight is nothing more than a great story. That it almost never has to do with this fighter's credentials. It's about telling a good story.

> "A great promoter is just a great Storyteller."

The Bad Guy was born.

Now retired, Sonnen reflected on his life and career on the Flagrant 2 podcast with Andrew Shulz.[4]

He spoke in depth about his decision to tell his story as a heel in his industry.

If you're asking what a Heel is, think about Hollywood. Sonnen notes that there are only two characters in Hollywood, a good guy and a bad guy. A heel and a face.

The heel plays the villain, the antagonist, the bad guy to the face's, hero, good guy persona. They are the yin and the yang of classic storytelling. Opposing forces ever at odds. The precarious battle for power between them always hanging in the balance.

In the fight game, selling a fight and getting attention is the essential role of the heel.

A fight must have a purpose. There must be something at stake. Something worth paying attention to (a mission or a vision).

This purpose must be clear to the audience. Purpose is best shared in the form of a story that the audience can connect with. To Sonnen, you must be yourself at all times – or at least be in character – to connect with the audience.

Each fighter – in our case, entrepreneur, founder, manager – must decide which character to play.

Do you want to be the heel of the industry or the face? No answer is right or wrong – it's what works for you. Once you pick a side, though, you MUST stay there.

Sonnen refers to this as a fierce adherence to one's code, even if it means breaking the "rules."

It's all about what's at stake.

Can your brand go beyond that? Sure. If you'd like it to. However, the best place to start is with building a deeper reputation for those you want to serve. Think about branding as the way to become known well by the people who matter in your industry. We'll tackle this exercise at the end of this chapter.

Here are three quick stats for your consideration:

- "Out of all business decision makers, 84 percent start their buying process with a referral. And Google is the very first place people look after getting a referral."[5]

- A referral is a story told about you to someone else in your market. Get your industry greats to tell stories about you and watch the volume of referrals increase.

- Next, "82% of people are more likely to trust a company when their senior executives are active on social media."[6]

  - Like it or not, social media is here to stay. Executives who use it as a tool to humanize themselves, their company and their mission build trust faster than those who don't. Which side of this equation do you want to be on?

- And lastly, "Only 33% of buyers trust messages from a company while almost 90% of customers trust recommendations from someone they know."[6]

  - Recommendations are key. Empower your audience to share relevant stories about you so that they know you'll help them tell their own stories better.

A brand is more than pictures, quotes and being self-important. Much more. We all need to remember that a brand is a promise. A promise of consistency, quality and adventure.

A brand can represent whatever aspects of you that you want. Branding is about speaking to the subconscious mind of your audience and getting them emotionally involved in the journey.

If you were to look at my brand, yes, I have pictures of myself. They're professional photographs. I'm invested in building a brand that promotes quality, positivity and creativity. I tell stories about my life and my experiences. I always relate my experiences back to a theme (see Chapter 2 for more on Theme) or value for the audience's benefit. Period.

To the untrained eye, it looks like I'm the main focal point of what I do, but actually I'm not. The MISSION I'm on is the center of my brand.

I am but a vessel to share the reminder that we are humans solving human problems in a business context. And that to lead, sell and live authentically, we must use story.

Street Vendor Storytelling

I've had the fortune to travel a fair amount in my career. One of my favorite activities to do while traveling is to go people-watching. I'll go to a town square or local market, sip a cup of tea and watch how the people move. It's fascinating. I watch how people communicate, how they build and how they sell.

I particularly enjoy watching street vendors build rapport with pedestrians. Street vendors have to get customers into their "stores." Their efforts to capture attention range from annoying to downright genius. Watching street vendors open conversations on the street is a fascinating experience to behold.

These vendors showcase their ability to draw on the stories we tell ourselves about who we are and how we want the world to perceive us. Street vendors are able to read people and drive them to action – fast.

Their technique of choice to coax you to open your wallet? The pattern interrupt. I found one of my favorite examples of this a few years ago, when I went to Istanbul, Turkey, to lead a series of sales workshops at a University Entrepreneurship Accelerator Program.

On one of the few days in which I had free time, I wanted to take advantage of my time in the historic city. I went for a long walk and wound up in a hilly neighborhood called the Galata Tower Square.

Perched atop of a hill in the neighborhood that bears its name, the Galata Tower is one of the famous peaks piercing the skyline of Istanbul. The tower is an homage to the many cultural influences in the region: a mix of Ottoman, Genoese and East Roman.

Depending on who you ask, the tower has a few important timelines. The first dates back to 528 AD. The Byzantium Empire Anastasios built the tower as a lighthouse. The Empire needed a lookout point against the siege of the Genoese.

The second dates back to 1348 AD. The Genoese repurposed the tower to serve as a surveillance outpost. (I bet you can tell that the tower didn't help the Byzantium Empire much against the Genoese).

From there, the tower became a fire detection outpost for the Ottomans and eventually a dungeon during the reign of Süleiman The Magnificent.

One of the most interesting stories about the tower, however, comes from the life and works of Hezarfen Ahmed Çelebi in 1638 AD. Çelebi constructed wings made of wood, jumped from the top of the tower and succeeded in flying all the way to Usküdar Doğancan, some four miles away. One of the first manned flights in history... predating the Wright Brothers by 268 years![7]

Aside from its storied past, the Tower is a beautiful piece of history. Well worth a visit. Which is how I happened upon it during my trip.

I arrived at the bottom of the hill and walked up the steep embankment. With every step, I could feel the age of the area. The buildings sit slotted tightly on slender winding streets. So slender in fact, that most cars wouldn't dare pass. Mid-morning commuters filled the streets. Walking up and down taking in the sights with the crisp morning air.

As I started my ascent, I took out my camera and I saw a gentleman with a shoeshine box walking down the hill toward me. The box was of typical Turkish design – wooden with a golden trim. The box doubled as both storage and as a platform from which the shiner might ply his trade.

The moment before he passed me, his shoe shining brush fell from its box. I heard the brush clatter on the pavement. The brush landed a few yards behind my feet. The shoe shiner continued on, unaware. I noticed and I was hesitant to mention it as I was about to get on my way and I didn't have much time.

I looked over at him and then I remembered The Golden Rule that my parents taught me: "Do unto others as you would have them do unto you." I called after the gentleman. Mind you, I speak zero Turkish. I made a veiled attempt to call after him with the word I believed to be "Hello." I shouted: "Merhaba," in his direction.

Spinning on a dime, the shoe shiner turned around. I pointed to his brush on the pavement. He hastened back to pick it up and made his way over to me. And with a pained smile on his face, he said to me in broken English: "Bless you! I feed my family with the shoes shine." Nodding, I gave him my best thumbs up and say, "Okay, great!" and I turned to go on my way.

Blocking my path, the shoe shiner perched atop his shoe shining box and offered to shine my shoes for free as a thank you. Politely, I declined his offer and made a move to leave. He cornered me again and insisted on shining my shoes. He said, "You give me back my work. I must thank you with a free shoes shine. It is Turkish way."

I declined again, because I had on a pair of brand new Vans and I didn't want my sneakers covered in anything. I started walking away for a third time. At that exact moment a window on the corner apartment three stories up, popped open.

A person started screaming at the man – in English – saying, "You always bother the tourists. Leave them alone.

Stop with dropping your brush trying to make them pay you!" During this verbal fracas, I made my escape. I proceeded up the hill, flabbergasted and inspired.

My sales brain started kicking over at what just happened. What an incredible method to generate leads! To be fair, I don't like this method because it relies on manipulation of the prospect – me. Playing on someone's honesty to get them to stop and use your services.

Now while manipulative in its intent, there is a certain genius to the structure of the tactic. The method relies on storytelling at its core.

Here's how:

Storytelling allows each of us "to drop the brush" in front of our audience, inspiring them to pick it up and bring it back. It invites the prospect to start the conversation themselves.

Storytelling connects on an emotional level. It's an important step to build the three key elements of buy-in: KLT – Know, Like and Trust. Buy-in, in this instance, means making a sale or rallying your team, or others toward a mission, cause or vision.

The shoe shiner played on the story I tell to myself about wanting to be honest and forthright – just like my parents taught me to be. He manipulated me into helping me tell my own story better... He reminded me of my brand.

I took action accordingly. While his tactics are a bit shady, they do share an important lesson about storytelling: The story must resonate with the individual for it to be effective and drive them to action.

Take a moment and write down a few thoughts in your *Superpower Storytelling Workbook* about how you could drop the brush for your audience.

Scan the QR Code with your phone!

* * * * *

A brand is a simple concept. A brand is nothing more than a promise. I'll agree that the term "Branding" is an overused these days. And I get it. This adds infinitely more friction to the idea of having a brand.

Here's the deal though: if you don't have a brand or you're not building one, you're allowing the market to decide who you are and what your value is. You give the market the opportunity to decide how to view you and to decide what your story is.

This becomes more important with our interactions becoming increasingly digital. I don't know about you, but I'd prefer not to give the market that much power over my image. And neither do you, that's why you're reading this book.

Look at tools like Open AI's Chat GPT. The tool gained one million users in five days.[8] The fastest tech tool to reach that coveted mark. For comparison, Twitter took 24 months, Facebook 10 months and Instagram 2.5 months.[9] At the time of this writing, Chat GPT has an estimated one billion monthly site visitors and 100 million active users and growing.[10]

The tool is nothing short of incredible. Its speed, clarity and breadth are scratching the surface of what's possible with AI. And just think, this is the worst the tool will ever be. It's a fascinating and scary time to be alive.

As a result of the tool, millions of "experts" will come online in the next few years. The "experts" will boast "knowledge" that they have little understanding of. Knowledge they never experienced or learned.

Their expertise will show a capacity to access a knowledge base and publish information. That doesn't make an expert. Nor does it prove a track record of understanding a subject or method.

In times like these, real experts with a proven track record will separate themselves. They'll rise to the top through their works and the stories they tell. Their brand will reflect this.

Building a brand is important these days and it starts with story. Once we know what stories to tell, then we work on delivery.

Remember how we discussed that the whole goal of story-telling is to help your audience better tell their own story? Now it's time to dive into one of the ways storytelling can help business owners build audiences.

The Importance of Storytelling

One of the key metrics of success in business these days is audience building. However, there's a misconception about audiences these days. The metric you'll hear marketers obsess over is reach: "How much reach will this post get?" or "What's the reach of your podcast?" or "What's the reach, reach, reach?" etc.,etc.

While reach is an important metric, it's a vanity metric. Sure you "reached" a few people with your message but the reason we leverage storytelling is because we strive for resonance. It's not enough to simply get in front of a large audience. The goal is to build an engaged one.

You can pick whichever one you like. I don't know about you, but I know which one I choose.

One of the best articles on the subject is Kevin Kelly's *1,000 True Fans.*[II]

Kevin Kelly – former Editor of Wired Magazine – penned this epic blog post back in 2007.

For context – the iPhone1 debuted that year, Facebook (Meta) exploded on the scene unseating MySpace (remember MySpace?) and Rihanna's Umbrella infected the airways peaking at #1 on the Billboard charts. Yep. That's a long time ago.

1000 True Fans is a quick read and full of value. Recommended reading for sure but for our purposes, I'll give you the TLDR.

If you have 1,000 people who love your work, you have the makings of building a sustainable business or a thriving community. The math works regardless of your vocation.

Let's dive into the numbers behind three scenarios.

- If we have 1,000 people paying us $100 a year ($8.33/month) we have a $100,000/year business. Not bad.

- If we have 1,000 people paying us $1,000 a year ($83 a month) we have a $1 million/year business. Pretty cool, huh?

- If we have 1,000 people paying us $10,000 a year we have a $10 million/year business.

You can see how this concept grows exponentially. By adjusting the price for your 1,000 true fans you can achieve massive growth. This works both financially and from a community perspective.

The important part about this though is not so much the price. It's about the number 1,000. The number 1,000 is important because it's not a huge number. We've all seen "influencers" or businesses with millions of followers. Seeing followings of that size, it can become a big mental exercise of "I'll never have that many followers," or "I'll never be able to have that many people care about my story," or "I'll never be able to turn my small following in to dollars."

Building an audience – something that should be exciting and fun – becomes an, "Is this even worth it?"

In fact. Yes it is.

Have you heard of Arii? Arianna Renee, better known by her handle @Arii is an Instagram influencer whose account boasts some 2.6 million followers. In 2019, Renee decided to start a clothing line. It failed miserably. How miserably? Renee wasn't able to meet the manufactures minimum production threshold of just 36 T-shirts sold to get her line produced.[12]

Let this serve as a reminder that "celebrity" and "reach" don't necessarily equal resonance. Just because people are watching doesn't mean you've captured their attention. You'll be fine.

That's why I love the sheer simplicity of the *1,000 True Fans* Framework.

First, you're able to wrap your head around what the number 1,000 is. You've likely touched $1,000 or you have 1,000 followers across your social media accounts or on your email list, etc. 1,000 – it's an approachable number.

Let's break it down even further.

Let's say you were to take the time to build relationships individually. It would take you about three years, talking to a brand new person each day to reach 1,000 people. (You could talk to three people a day and achieve the same in less than a year.) Now the big project of having 1,000 people to pay you $8 a month, $80 a month, or whatever your rate, is less daunting. That's perhaps my favorite part about the framework.

1,000 True Fans takes the opaque and it boils down to something attainable, i.e., I wanna have a $1 million business or I need to have an audience size of 100k to achieve my measure of success. It also makes the importance of storytelling clear. Getting to the magical number 1,000 starts with stories. Find your tribe by speaking directly to them.

It starts with your brand. Your brand starts with your promise. Your promise starts with who you are behind your business. That is what gets people to identify with you and say: "Yes! You're the person who understands me. I want to learn more about what you have to offer."

To be clear, it's okay if your audience size isn't in the tens or hundreds of thousands or even in the millions. We'd all love to get to that level. That's the whole reason for this book*.

Okay, let's be serious again. Building relationships with *1,000 True Fans* is all you need to ensure your success.

Do some quick math to back into the revenue number you want for yourself using this model. I guarantee that you're closer than you think. This is a great way to start looking at your audience with understanding.

Shameless plug - Follow me on social @stephensteers_ ;)

Here are some quick metrics that you can use to get one more true fan today. In one-to-three years' time, you'll see how doable it is. It requires the commitment of being you, telling the world about yourself and what you're up to. Or leaving it up to the market to decide who you are. The choice is yours.

It doesn't require a huge amount of time. All it takes is consistency. Consistency is the silver bullet.

* * * * *

Let's step back into the branding sector for a moment.

The most important part of a brand is the subconscious emotion it conjures in the audience. Activation of the subconscious further illuminates the importance of storytelling. In order to conjure relevance in the subconscious, you need to show up for yourself first.

How do you show up for yourself?

By putting yourself out there. Talking about what you do and inviting people to have conversations about it. Sharing stories about what you do and why it's important to your audience = growth. 100% assured. When you show up for yourself, it's proof that you can show up for your clients, for your family and for those around you. The stories are the cords of your brand that people are going to attach to.

Let's take a deeper look into the importance of storytelling for your business. Regardless of who you are, what you do, or your goals, if you aren't building a brand, it will mean trouble for you in the coming years.

Here are some quick statistics on branding to set the tone: 90% of the video, audio, photo, and text-based content consumed today by Gen Z is created by individuals, NOT corporations.[13] Let that sink in for a second. Damn near 100% of the content consumed by a whole generation is created by individuals.

Gen Z are those born between 1997-2012, which would make them between 11 and 17 years of age at the time of this writing. There are a host of reasons why Gen Z – the most connected generation – who grew up with the internet, prefers viewpoints of the individual.

One important note is if we look at the world, the classic institutions that Millennials, Gen X and Boomers had deep trust for are eroding.

Banks are failing left and right, government is centralizing and a college degree isn't worth what it used to be in the job market.

Gen Z is in flux and have taken to the internet to fashion their lives. They trust the individual and are driven by values. 86 percent of consumers say that authenticity is a key factor when deciding what brands they like and support. [13]

You might say to yourself, "I don't work with Gen Z. This means nothing to me or my business." And that's exactly the wrong way of thinking.

You may not have anything to do with them now. But what about ten years from now? They'll all be of prime working age – which means you may hire from this generation when they have an increased share of influence and buying power. Furthermore, having a great brand can bring the expenses related to hiring and training down by as much as 50%.[14]

If you want your business to exist and to grow exponentially, this is the group that's going to keep you in prime position to win over the coming decades.

Let's dive even deeper:

89% of buyers stay loyal to brands that share their values.[13] This works for both B2B and B2C. Brand loyalty manifests itself as buyers returning to the brand over and over again, sharing the brand with others and representing a brand with satisfaction. How will a shopper know if a brand shares its values? By the branding and the stories shared by the brand, of course.

77% of B2B marketers say branding is crucial for growth.[14] Using this stat as our launch point, it's clear to see that branding is important for building loyalty and connection with prospects.

Physics, the governing scientific principles of the universe, has a law called entropy. The law of entropy states that there are no static forces in the universe. You're either growing and improving or you are decaying and shrinking.

If you're not building, you're breaking. Period. There's chaos and there's order, both attainable through motion but there is no middle ground left in today's marketplace. If you don't have a brand or are not building one yet, you're seeding market share to your competition. No matter which way you slice it.

Deciding Your Storytelling Path

There are two schools of thought that we should break down before you decide which direction to go in. Everyone has an opinion. Everyone has a direction. You need one as well.

If you are part of School A:

You're a new entrepreneur or a freelancer. You're launching your first company. You're looking to establish yourself and raise your profile in the marketplace. You're thinking about your story and haven't used it yet. If that's you, there's a great opportunity to start writing your narrative.

This will work well for you because you're starting fresh. And I know It sounds intimidating and scary, but to become an authority, it all starts with consistency. If you want to be a thought leader in your market, you won't have to unlearn bad habits to be effective. But you're new, so you can start with what works: the art of storytelling.

If you are a part of School B:

School B is for the veterans in the room. You've been around for a while, have won a few customers and you're making a good amount of money each year. You're thinking about how to take it to the next level because things are stagnant.

You don't know what to put out there, what it's going to look like or what people will think or feel (or insert your own fear here). I get it. I've been there too. There are lots of ways to approach these fears. It's my job to give you the tools, tips and tactics to make storytelling in business your newest superpower.

I hear from my clients all the time that they're "uncomfortable" putting themselves out there. They tell me that they're not looking for the limelight or for attention and cite two main objections about putting themselves out there: fear of judgment and lack of preparation.

Fear Of Judgment

The first is that you have a fear of judgment – for who you are, for what you're going to say or for your delivery. Let's call a spade a spade. Your fear of sharing about your life, business or customers comes from a fear of judgment. Plain and simple.

Take a breath and acknowledge this. You're the one telling yourself that people are going to judge you. The truth is that no one is thinking about you enough to judge you. They're thinking about themselves and their own lives.

Let's take a step back and remember that no one actually cares about your message until you give them a reason to. This doesn't happen overnight. This is the first step in getting started and keeping consistent.

Secondly, you're being selfish. You've been through a lot in your life and business career. The world needs more authentic leadership. Keeping your story to yourself is doing a disservice to the world and isn't helping anyone.

Lack Of Preparation

If we're able to better prepare, we'll automatically have less fear of judgment. We must remember the importance of storytelling: we're helping our audience to tell their own story better. Remembering this allows our emotions to take a backseat. Or at least stand a bit further afield of the initial fear.

This way we're able to put the story at the forefront – blocking the feelings of judgment – through the use of story. We'll illustrate this point further when we discuss The Five Elements of *Storytelling* in Chapter 2.

Each of these elements enables the audience to find their own place in the action.

Yes, the stories are from our lives, businesses and experiences, but every story is 100% built to share lessons with our audience so they can see the parity in themselves.

Storytelling is less about us – the messenger. It's all about the audience. Every story is and should be about your audience.

It's the same thing with your brand. Do you want to invite people to experience who you are? To become members of an exclusive club? Are you the all access company that welcomes all comers?

Are you the type of brand that's fun and quirky or are you more serious?

There's no right or wrong answer. It's what works for you.

The question is simple: Are you summoning your people to come and find you? Are you sounding the sweet drums of celebration in the distant jungles? Are you welcoming your tribe back home?

Are you cutting through the noise of the marketing quagmire? Story is the bridge to get them into the boat. Tell your story, show your results. It's how each of us can get to know, like and trust a brand or a person. Branding, storytelling and growing a business are all about building trust quickly.

Whether you use their products or services, brands are consistent across markets. Some great brand storytelling examples are Hilton, WeWork and McDonalds.

Have you ever visited a WeWork, eaten at a McDonalds or spent the night at a Hilton Hotel? Each of these multinational brands boast thousands of locations all over the world. If you've visited any of them, you've seen the consistency of their branding.

Design elements, level of service and the quality of the experience, etc. The markers of the brand are evident. The story is the same whether you're in Mumbai, India or Scottsdale, Arizona. The expectations are set.

When we visit these places we have an idea of what to expect. We know the story that the brand is telling us and we know how we relate to it.

> WeWork – Strong internet, a steady supply of coffee and a community of entrepreneurs.

> McDonalds – Fast Food, Open Late,
> Ronald McDonald

> Hilton Hotels – A great night's sleep, top notch service with comfort and style.

These brands have grown for exactly that reason. People are able to count on them no matter where they are in the world. We can count on these brands to help us tell the story we need to make our lives better.

You can do the same thing. Branding yourself, with your stories gives you a unique space in the market.

Remember, no one's going to find you on their own. In the words of Christopher Charles Hampton, "It doesn't pay to be the world's best kept secret."

Now that we know the importance of communicating our ideas and what storytelling can do for our businesses, lets dive into what a story actually is.

Storytelling Exercise

Open up you *Superpower Storytelling Workbook* and take notes.

Get your workbook here:

Scan the QR Code with your phone!

CHAPTER 2

What is a Story?

What stories actually are, how they work and how they're structured to change our brains

Before we get to what Storytelling is, let me tell you a little story.

It's the 1960s, in Eugene, Oregon, USA. A track and field athlete from the University of Oregon by the name of Phil Knight with the help of his Coach Bill Bowerman created a small sportswear startup called Blue Ribbon Sports.[15] [16]

Blue Ribbon Sports (BRS) originally served as a distributor for the Japanese shoe brand Onitsuka Tiger. Knight and Bowerman would sell shoes out of the back of Phil's car at track meets, netting $8,000 in their first year and $20,000 the following year. Sensing an opportunity, the pair opened their first storefront in Santa Monica, California, in 1965. By 1967, BRS had a bi-coastal footprint when they expanded distribution and retail operations to Wellesley, Massachusetts.

After splitting with Onitsuka Tiger and seeing their business beginning to scale, Knight and Bowerman chose to rename their company, originally looking to call the company Dimension Six. However, as fate would have it, BRS' first key salesman, Jeff Johnson, had a suggestion. In a dream he saw the name of the Greek Goddess of Victory – Nike. He suggested the name to Knight and Bowerman.

On May 30, 1971, Nike was officially born. Their signature Waffle Trainer debuted with the now globally familiar Swoosh logo. They were looking to scale their business and bring their innovative shoe designs to the world.

Nike proceeded through the 1970s taking more and more market share. But it wasn't until the 1980s that they really hit stride (pun fully intended).

In the early 1980s, executives from Nike courted a young basketball player out of UNC by the name of Michael Jeffery Jordan. Some, including myself, call him the greatest basketball player of all time.

If you disagree, you can fight me about it in your written review of this book ;). Nike execs loved Jordan and knew he was special. They decided to sponsor him, offering a signature shoe line and a $250k contract – a princely sum in those days (equivalent to $723,869.10 in 2023 dollars).

Back in the 1980s, NBA teams had strict uniform requirements, i.e., [players] "must wear shoes that not only matched their uniforms, but matched the shoes worn by their teammates."[17] Further, the shoe must be at least 51% white. A rule that the NBA only changed in the late 2000s.[18]

On October 18, 1984, during his sixth preseason game at Madison Square Garden, Michael Jordan debuted his signature sneaker. Black and red in color, the Air Jordan 1 shoe flouted the NBA's uniformity requirements – drawing the ire of league officials.

Nike executives received a strongly-worded letter about their lack of compliance. The NBA made it plain that this wasn't got to fly. The NBA fined Michael $5k every time he stepped on the court for wearing the shoes. Legend has it that Jordan continued to wear the shoes with no regard for the rules. Birthing his legendary career and his multi-billion dollar shoe empire.

However, you'd be wrong; well, at least partially. Jordan never wore the black shoes in an official game. However, in a stroke of marketing genius, execs at Nike seized the opportunity.

Nike crafted a campaign showing the stylish Michael as the supreme athlete dominating the competition while sporting a gold chain and his banned signature shoe. As he ran back down court, the camera focused on the shoes and covered them in a giant X. Saying that the NBA banned the shoes.

Sales. Went. Crazy.

The $65 shoe ($185 in today's money – shout out to inflation for keeping up!) and the Nike/Jordan brand as we know it today was born.

Nike was the brand of the rebels. Those who found themselves on the outside of tradition and wanted to show the world. Nike helped each of those rebels tell their own story better. Giving every rebel a uniform.

And in a few decades an otherwise unknown sportswear company became a multi-billion brand, the home of many of the worlds top athletes and sportswear brand of choice for millions all over the world.

* * * * *

Ok, so what is Storytelling?

Storytelling exemplifies the human spirit. Storytelling is an art. It's a unique art in that it doubles as a science. We use storytelling to entertain, to build rapport and to share knowledge. Stories are formulaic, which means we can all learn and grasp techniques to improve how we live in our world.

Stories are the glue that hold us together. They're also the fabric of commerce. From the home you live in, all the way down to the cup of coffee you're sipping as you read this, a story led to the sale.

Commerce happens because people believe that investing in a good or service will yield a positive return. The belief that their purchase will provide greater value to their life or business than the cost of the good or service. In essence, the purchase of a good or service will better help them tell their own story.

EV's, Watches and First Class Flights

What kind of car do you drive?

Drivers of a Toyota Prius or a Tesla buy these vehicles – at least in part – to fill the gaps of the story they want to tell the world about themselves or their business, i.e., that there's an interest in environmental issues. The driver enjoys the perception of being a Prius or a Tesla owner.

The Toyota Prius

Before Teslas started to dominate the road in the EV market, in the early 2000s, Toyota produced a car called the Prius. Not much of a car to look at and the performance? Worse.

The Toyota Prius is a popular hybrid car sold in over 90 markets around the world. It's the first mass produced Hybrid vehicle, implementing a combination of gas and electric power.

As of September 2022, the Prius has over five million units sold globally, winning the vehicle the noted distinction of top selling hybrid car in the world.

The Prius owes its success to two primary markets. The United States and Japan.

However, the origins of its popularity are somewhat controversial. In the early 2000s, the Prius became a status symbol. Two seemingly unrelated factions adopted the Prius as their patron saint:

- Progressive celebrities who sought to bring attention to environmental issues. Their efforts helped the vehicle earn the nickname "The Hollywood Car."[19]

- To further prove that heaven has a sense of humor, the Prius also appealed to staunch conservatives in the USA. Their draw to the vehicle was for its fuel efficiency.[20] (2001 models boasted 42mpg city and 41mpg highway with current models 54mpg city and 50mpg highway). In their eyes, the Prius' fuel efficiency helped to diminish the U.S. dependence on foreign oil. This group even earned their own nickname "Prius Patriots."[21]

Yet, there are hybrid car advocates who like the Prius for more practical reasons. For example, former CIA Chief R. James Woolsey Jr. drives a Prius because of its low fuel consumption. Stating that it is a patriotic obligation to do so. By driving more efficient vehicles, Americans can reduce their support for foreign oil. It's hard to argue with energy independence.

Even today, fuel efficiency remains an important factor for purchasing the Prius.

However, data from CNW Marketing Research shines a different light. One of the main reasons for buying the Prius is the statement it makes about the driver's personal values. Enter the term "Prius Politics."

Prius Politics is a phenomenon where the desire to appear environmentally conscious is strong. In fact, it's a stronger buying motivator than actually reducing greenhouse gas emissions. In essence, the story wins out.

The product tells the story for the owner. Helping the owner better tell their own story and share that story with others. Oh yeah, and the driver gets to save the environment at the same time.

Luxury Watches

Do you wear a watch? I wear a mid-range Casio. It's low key, comfortable and can take a beating. The purpose of my watch is to tell the time.

Some folks who wear watches choose to buy a Rolex, Patek Phillippe, or other brands that I can't begin to afford – yet. If watch ownership was simply about telling the time, watch collectors or owners of these storied brands could save tens if not hundreds of thousands of dollars and buy a Timex, Casio or a Seiko watch instead.

Some might even say that Timex, Casio and Seiko watches have more functionality. Not to mention, Timex, Casio and Seiko watches tell the time, don't need to be stored in a safe when you're not wearing them and won't cause an international incident if they're lost or stolen. In other words, they're infinitely more practical.

However, purchasing a Rolex, Patek Philippe or Chopard isn't about telling the time. Buying one of these watches is about buying into the prestige and tradition of hand craftsmanship. Ownership of such time pieces provides access to a unique club. A club where relationship building with other watch collectors, a demonstration of financial ability, and perhaps a demonstration of your exquisite taste in watches are the currency.

Let's not forget to mention that watches hold their value well over time (pun not intended, of course). Ownership of an expensive watch says something about the owner of said watch. The watch enables the owner to tell and live out a story they have for themselves.

First Class Flights

Flying first class is another example.

You may be 6'2" (1.90m) as I am and actually need extra space on an airplane (my knees ache just thinking about it). But the experience of flying first class is what makes it desirable.

Let's break it down.

First class ticket holders board before everyone else. All other passengers board to see the first class patrons sitting "comfortably" without a care in the world.

You see them chowing down on shrimp cocktails and unlimited champagne in lay-flat seats, while you chase a serving of pretzels with cranberry juice from your middle seat near the aft bathroom in coach.

If it were about efficiency, the airlines would load the plane from back to front. The first class patrons would spend the least amount of time on the plane. They'd be the last on and the first off. They'd get the privacy of not having to deal with the economy flyers at all... but we all know that's not how it works.

As comfortable as flying first class is, it screams "attention" more than it screams comfort (flights from North America to Asia, not withstanding – comfort is essential on flights that long). First class seats help their patrons tell a story of status.

Think for a moment about some of the folks you've seen flying first class. Many questions pop into your head: Who are they? What do they do? Where are they coming from? How can I fly first class?

The idea of flying first class becomes emotional and for some, aspirational. You get the point.

The examples above show how brands leverage story to increase the desirability of their goods and services and charge premium prices. The process starts with listening. Listening to the stories customers want to tell about themselves.

When we start with listening, we then know the outcomes our ideal audience wants. When we know what the audience wants, we're able to extend that outcome into every story detail. When we extend the outcome into a story we build trust. Trust that our brand can help our patrons achieve their desired outcome.

Now that we've seen a few brands use story to tug at the heart strings of their customers, let's dissect how. We'll view these through The Five Elements of Storytelling.

The Five Elements of Storytelling[22]

Every story is the same. The exact same. Well, the good ones are at least...

Think of the stories in great ad campaigns (Dos Equis' *"The Most Interesting Man in The World,"* and the *"Got Milk?"* ads of the 1990s) or of Shakespeare's *Romeo and Juliet* or David Simon's *The Wire*.

Each of these is a prime example of a great storytelling. Each of them is the exact same.

What do I mean?

Each example is memorable, conjures emotions and contains the same key story elements.

Character

The first important element of the story is character. Character, in this case, isn't simply what you do when no one is watching or a set distinctive personality traits of an individual. It's more about the important individuals, objects or protagonists involved in the story. These are the people, places and objects involved in pushing the story forward.

You can think of characters as people, places and even inanimate objects. A character drives the action of the story forward. Whether it's a character with a big or small role all depends on the story you want to tell.

No story is worth its weight if it can't captivate an audience with its characters. If you're writing a story, characters are how you get the dialogue or the conversations moving to tell the story. Make sense?

Now let's move onto element number two:

Conflict

There is no story without conflict. Conflict is what happens in the story. It's the problem, the challenge, the difficulty. It's the issue(s) that need solving. It's what keeps us locked into what's happening and it's an integral part of what builds emotion in audiences.

Conflict is what's at stake for our character(s).

Once a story establishes characters, and the other three elements, we get to learn the conflict. Conflict usually takes place in ACT TWO of a play.

ACT TWO in a play – think Shakespeare – is when things go crazy. It's when an incisive moment of drama occurs. Something happens that changes the course of the set up.

Conflicts always need resolution. Resolution usually takes place by ACT THREE. Which helps keep the audience emotionally rooted in the story.

There are many different ways to think about conflict. Conflict in storytelling can take many forms. It all depends on context, i.e., sharing stories in marketing, to rally your team to a revenue goal or to handle sales objections.

The most common kinds of conflict are internal and external. Internal conflict can take the form of a mental block, anxiety or some form of self-doubt in a main character. External conflicts come in the form of professional challenges, pending deadlines, bullies, etc. – things the character has no control over.

In Chapter 3 – *The Superpower Storytelling Framework* – we'll discuss the three types of stories you already have and how to use them to establish conflict in context.

Plot

The plot is what actually happens in the story. Plot is all the elements that comprise the story.

A plot contains a series of events that lead to expression of conflict. These include climax, rising action, falling action and resolution of the story.

In Shakespeare's terms, that's our Act Three. A well-structured plot will – we hope – tie up the loose ends that happen throughout a story. If loose ends aren't tied up, the audience is left confused. (I'm talking to you Jeffrey Lieber, J.J. Abrams, and Damon Lindelof – even after seven years, I still don't know what *LOST* was about.)

Stories can leverage multiple plots as well. Some stories center around a timeline. Starting at the end and taking the story through the events that led up to that final action – think of flashbacks. (Christopher Nolan's film *Memento* is a great example.)

Setting

One of the most important and often less appreciated elements of story is the setting. Setting is where a story takes place. The setting can be a physical place or a time in history.

To make setting an effective element we need to describe where the action is taking place, i.e., the story takes place in the office at your very first job or when you were a child in the '70s, '80s, '90s, etc.

The period the story takes place in can be its own setting. Period specific details like technology or clothing can help draw the audience in. Leveraging descriptive language about setting transports the audience directly into the story.

Now we move on to the fifth element: theme.

Theme

Theme is the main idea or the lesson of your story. The theme is what you want the audience to gain from whatever you're sharing with them.

Theme is the thesis of your story. The main takeaway. It's what you want the audience to use in their own lives or in their own business. Theme is how we get our audience to ask questions like:

- Am I prepared for this?
- Do I know enough?
- Can I make a good choice?
- Can I handle this on my own?

That's why you're going to tell a story. The goal is to provide a lesson and to open up a conversation. A conversation that makes it easy for deep connection with your audience. That's the power of a strong theme.

Now you know The Five Elements of Story (character, conflict, plot, setting and theme). When they're done well, incredible story arcs come to life and create one of the most relatable story archetypes known to human kind: the Hero's Journey.

The Hero's Journey is a story that lives in all our hearts and minds. The key to deploying the elements of story in your own storytelling journey is all about context. The context of storytelling for your life or for business will differ – slightly.

Let's discuss that structure a bit more.

Storytelling Structure

Structure is the frame upon which storytelling rests. Structure contains the key elements that make a good story. You've seen it in almost every superhero, action film or romantic comedy. Here are the three stages of the hero's journey as coined by academic Joseph Campbell in 1949:[23]

1. **Act One:** The Departure Act: the Hero leaves the ordinary world.

2. **Act Two:** The Initiation Act: the Hero ventures into the unknown. The Hero arrives in the "Special World" where, through trials and challenges they are reborn a champion.

3. **Act Three:** The Return Act: the Hero returns in triumph.

The Hero's journey usually consists of three acts divided into 12 essential steps. Our Hero experiences each of these 12 steps to make a transformation that draws us in. Chris Vogler, outlines these 12 steps in his book *Monolith*.

I'm going to define and outline the 12 steps of the hero's journey using a common film that you've most likely seen.

For our example, we'll use the 1999 blockbuster film *The Matrix* starring Keanu Reeves.

The Matrix is a trendsetting cult classic and one of the coolest films from my adolescence. The film deploys The Hero's Journey with purpose and alacrity. You'll know each stage when you see it.

1. The Ordinary World

Establishing a baseline "normal." What was life like before the transformation? It could be dark, boring or uncomfortable. This is where we meet our main character – our hero. This is the time before the hero's journey starts.

The Matrix: This is where we learn Neo is a hacker with a day job.

2. The Call of Adventure

After establishing the day-to-day life of our hero, a catalyst appears to take the main character out of their comfort zone to set them on their path to herodom.

The Matrix: Neo sees some suspicious patterns in computer code. He posts online looking for answers and happens to get a message from Trinity who claims to know how Neo can find the answers he seeks.

3. Refusal of the Call

The hero learns that adventure and significant challenges await. You'd think they'd start right off on their journey and you'd be wrong. The hero is reluctant to get started for fear of the obstacles that will certainly arise.

The Matrix: Neo arranges to meet Trinity. While meeting, the two are beset by "Agents" who attempt to capture them. Neo is unfortunately captured and tortured. He believes his capture a nightmare and no longer wishes to continue his search.

4. Meeting the Mentor

The hero eschews the reluctance and decides to learn more about the adventure that lies ahead. The hero's inexperience with the challenge makes them unfit to prevail without some kind of help. That's when a guide or mentor shows up to steward the hero through their journey by providing their experience, training and wisdom.

The Matrix: Even through Neo's reluctance, Trinity persuades Neo to meet Morpheus. Morpheus explains the landscape, the reasoning, the emotions and the path forward. Morpheus invites Neo to his calling, giving him the choice between enlightenment or going back to his ordinary life.

5. Crossing the First Threshold

There's a full-on decision to take up the mantle and go on the journey. The hero commits to their journey.

The Matrix: Confronted with the reality that there's more to the world than he has classically thought. In the famous scene with a raging storm outside, Morpheus offers Neo the choice of the blue pill, to go back to life as normal or the red pill to "see how deep the rabbit hole goes." Neo accepts Morpheus' offer of the red pill. Neo understands that now, there is no chance to turn back.

6. Tests, Allies, Enemies

This is what happens when the hero realizes the challenges they're up against and teams up with like-minded folks who share the same mission.

The Matrix:

Tests: Morpheus and Trinity introduce Neo to the Oracle, a prophet who foretold the existence of "The One" – a person who would come to open the eyes of humanity. In conversation with her, Neo is told that he isn't who everyone thinks he is.

Allies: Neo officially teams up with Morpheus and Trinity. Neo understands that the world is all a computer simulation and his purpose is to wake people up.

Enemies: Once Neo becomes awakened, Agent Smith becomes more persistent in his pursuit of Neo and his rebel gang.

7. Approach to the Inmost Cave

The hero can see that their goal is close.

The Matrix: After The Oracle tells Neo that he is not "The One," he is beset with confusion and lack of confidence. He needs to make a choice about what type of life he wants for himself.

8. The Ordeal

The Big Test. The hero faces their most difficult and challenging test so far.

The Matrix: While visiting with the Oracle, Cypher, a crew member of the rebel gang, betrays the rebels in exchange for a comfortable life in the Matrix. Cypher kills two rebel crew members and announces Neo, Trinity and Morpheus' presence to the Agents who storm Neo's meeting with the Oracle.

9. Reward (Seizing the Sword)

The hero realizes through their biggest challenges that the accomplishment they seek is within reach.

The Matrix: Agents capture Morpheus. Trinity and Neo narrowly escape the Matrix. Neo resigns himself to go back and rescue Morpheus from the agents.

10. The Road Back

The accomplishment that seemed close is actually further than imagined. Their spirit is buoyed and this is the start of what our friend Shakespeare would call our Act Three.

The Matrix: Trinity insists on coming with Neo to rescue Morpheus. Neo regains confidence in his abilities and starts to demonstrate skills that rival those of The Agents. Neo and Trinity successfully rescue Morpheus and return to their ship.

11. Resurrection

The hero rises to the occasion and becomes who they thought they could be.

The Matrix: Agent Smith ambushes and kills Neo before he's able to join Morpheus and Trinity on the ship. Trinity professes her love for Neo, reviving him. Neo awakens with new found abilities and destroys Agent Smith. The other agents flee in fear.

12. Return with the Elixir

The hero achieves the goal. They are whole. They have suffered and are now finally victorious.

The Matrix: Neo returns to the Matrix once more. He picks up a telephone and tells the machines that he will show all of their captives "a world where anything is possible."

These are the stages of the hero's journey broken down to the 12 essential steps. This is how great stories are built and this is why the resonate so strongly.

The Matrix remains one of the most influential films to this day. It birthed an entirely new style of storytelling and a whole new experience driven by strong editing. Further, its critical acclaim and financial success birthed a partnership for the Wachowski Brothers and Warner Bros. Films. *The Matrix* became a four-movie franchise grossing nearly $1.8 billion at the box office worldwide.[24]

* * * * *

Whether we're talking Nike Air Jordan's, EV's', luxury watches or first class travel, stories have a clear structure that invite audiences to see themselves in the action. It's our job to tell stories that welcome them.

Now it's time to dive into the *Superpower Storytelling Framework* and learn which stories we have to tell.

CHAPTER 3

The Superpower
Storytelling Framework

Know what stories you have, how they fit in
context and how to share them authentically,
so that you're the most interesting
person in the room

I t's Tuesday morning. You're up early. You make your way
to the kitchen and put on a pot of coffee to start your
day. French roast. Your favorite.

The coffee maker hums, cycling its process to create your
favorite life-giving elixir. While the coffee machine does its
thing, you walk into your home office.

Taking a seat at your desk, you log in to your computer and check your email. Wading through the plethora of spam, your heart skips a beat when you see a reply from an industry podcast.

You quickly click and open the email.

And to your surprise, they're offering you a guest spot on their show! Recording date is set for two weeks. The initial jolt of excitement quickly turns to dread. You have no idea what you're going to say on this podcast that will make you sound interesting...

You know you can't sit for an hour and pitch your services because that'd be poor form... but what are you gonna do?

Fear not! That's exactly what the Super Power Storytelling Framework will help you to master.

* * * * *

Why is storytelling a superpower?

Storytelling is a Superpower because it conjures emotions and memories within your audience. Storytelling sets the audience on the path toward remembering their own lives. The following framework is designed to make it easy for you to share stories and to add accessibility to your brand.

A brand that the world needs right now.

To set the tone I'd like to share this excerpt from Comedian Andrew Schulz – who took the world by storm during the pandemic in conversation – with modern intellectual Dr. Jordan B. Peterson.

However you feel about these two controversial characters, the following conversation is a perfect corollary to what this book is all about: *The Magic of Storytelling*. And whether you like either Dr. Peterson, Schulz or neither, they've done something correct. They've each successfully built an audience by helping many people tell their own stories better.

This excerpt outlines storytelling and its power:[25]

Andrew Shulz:

> *"We have a theory – I think we have a biological reaction to stories in the same way we have to music. I notice when I'm hanging out with my friends that I've known for decades we will retell the same stories we were all a part of and every single time our eyes light up, and we get goosebumps, we laugh and we get excited and the stories will morph and change and we get to relive them in the same way when a song comes on that was a song you absolutely loved or you were going through something, you get to feel all of those emotions again like you tap into them.*
>
> *"Even when someone tells a story in a group, it's different than when someone has a hot take or a premise. 'Hey, this thing happened.' Everybody shuts up. And all of a sudden, we're all around the campfire for some reason."*

Dr. Jordan Peterson:

> *"We see the world through a story. If you're out with your friends and you're telling a shared story, then you're liter-*

ally building the shared set of assumptions that constitute the friendship.

"If you're ensconced in a good story, then what you're doing is playing. The right story to tell is one that enables people to play along. These stories share something about who one of us is or who we all are.

"There's a reason why the Bible didn't just say do these things. There's a reason why they put them in stories; because it's far more impactful to listen to a story. I wonder if through osmosis the behavior in the stories kind of gets locked into our long-term memory; whereas, if you just tell someone a rule, it just short-term and may be fleeting.

"The thing about having a rule embodied in a story is you see how it's acted out. It's much more convincing to watch how something is acted out, partly because you know how to act it out. If it's just a rule you have to translate the rule into action. If it's a story, then the actions are laid out for you."

From this conversation we can see that humans have a biological reaction to stories in a manner similar to that of music.

When retelling stories with friend or colleagues, the shared experience evoke emotions and memories akin to listening to one's favorite song. There is a frequency change in the human psyche when storytelling comes into play.

Stories create a shared set of assumptions that underpin relationships, conduct and behavioral lessons, thus allowing the audience to see how lessons play out in direct action. Rules of conduct are easy to ignore or forget. Seeing as 65-70% of information is remembered when shared in story form,[26] story creates a more memorable way to share information in a way that the audience can play along and find belonging.

Think about a person who you admire: a leader from your career, your best friend or a family member. You more than likely love some of the stories they tell. You've heard them say the same story many times over the years but you don't tire of hearing it. That's story is now part of your life.

And every time you think about it, it extends the brand of your relationship. The ties that bind you together. They are your personal brand in action.

Your Leadership Brand

Yes, we're going to cover personal brands. Stick with me for a second though. As ugly as that term sounds, having a personal brand is a huge benefit.

A personal brand gives each of us a chance to be more accessible to our audiences. Authenticity enables who we are to shine brighter than what we do. It's much easier to invite people into what we do when they're familiar with who we are.

If you want to be a real leader in your company and in your industry for that matter, a personal brand is the ticket. It's also a surefire way to attract quality talent and build a company culture you can be proud of. Of course talent wants to work for an interesting company that does challenging work under strong leadership.

But 100% of the time, talent wants to work for a company with a great leader with whom they can identify. Storytelling is the difference maker here.

Case in point with Rob Campbell and Steve Jobs. Campbell is currently the CEO of Voalte. Voalte is provider of wireless software to hospitals and point-of-care facilities.

Back in 1977, however, Campbell, a budding programmer, sought his fortune in the up and coming personal computer space.

He decided to apply at the most well known companies in the space – the perfect vantage point for the coming personal computer revolution.

Campbell visited with one of the first companies on his list: Tandy Computers. He asked the executives pointedly, "What is your vision for the personal computer?" Their response flattened his enthusiasm. They replied: "We think it could be the next big thing on everyone's wish list for the holiday season!" Campbell left and continued his search.

Campbell's next stop was Commodore International. Commodore went on to become a publicly traded company. They created one of the most popular personal computers of all time – The Commodore 64. In 1977, they were a growing concern in the personal computer space. Their shares trading south of $1 per share.

Campbell met with the Commodore executive team. Campbell posed the same question: "What is your vision for the personal computer?"

Their replay was equally as deflating as Tandy's: "We think it could help our stock rise above $2 a share."

His enthusiasm waning, Campbell decided to accept a lunch invitation from a guy named Steve Jobs.

Campbell arrived at the lunch meeting and immediately noted Job's long hair and Birkenstocks. As they ordered, Campbell posed the same question to Jobs. "What is your vision for the personal computer?"

Campbell cites this meeting with Jobs as a sea change in his journey. He claims that Steve's answer still gives him goosebumps all these years later.

> "For the next hour, [Jobs] talked about how personal computers were going to change the world. He painted a picture of how it would change everything about the way we worked, educated our children and entertained ourselves. You couldn't help but buy in."

Steve Jobs was a magical storyteller whose vision captivated great talent. This is part and parcel to why Apple is so successful today.[27]

So we have to think about storytelling in a few buckets:

- As a way to build credibility in the marketplace (Authority Building and Thought Leadership)

- Creating a destination for people to grow in their careers and as human beings
  (Create culture, recruit talent)
- As a means to get the market excited to buy your products or services (Lead generation)

The holy grail of these three story types is the capacity to combine them into one. A singular story that shows agency. Leadership is having a clear mission, an actionable vision and awareness of the milestones that got you there. Then making each of those present in everything the company does.

One of my favorite examples of combining these types of stories is from a former client – a company named CertfID. Their mission is to detect and prevent wire transfer fraud.

One day, I asked their founder Tom why he decided to start his company. He shared the following: "I found an amazing new house that I wanted to buy. I did my research on it. It was in the perfect neighborhood, the price was competitive and it was the right size for my family's needs.

> "We fell in love with it and knew we had to make an offer. The owner accepted our offer and a few days later, I wired the $185,000 down payment to lock it in. My family and I were starting to get excited about the prospect of the next phase of our lives.

> "Unfortunately, the wire was intercepted by some unscrupulous characters. They stole the entire payment.

"I called my bank. I called my realtor. I showed up anywhere I could think of to get some help. I went through all the channels to report the wire fraud. Unfortunately, my bank and my realtors informed me that there was nothing they could do. There was no way to get the payment back.

"Adding further insult to injury, we weren't going to get the house. This infuriated me to no end. Like how does this happen? Why isn't there a better way to do this?

"After doing some digging, I learned that this was a big problem for home buyers. I discovered that there weren't any solutions in the market for this problem. So I started this company to make sure that no one else ever has to go through what me and my family did."

A tough and gut wrenching experience to be sure, but what a story! You can instantly relate to the painful emotions Tom experienced with the loss of money AND of his family's dream home.

You can also get onboard with his attitude of taking charge and creating a product to prevent what happened to him from happening to anyone else in the future. This difficult experience builds immediate trust with Tom and his team. And today CertifID currently protect billions of dollars and enable trustworthiness across transactions big and small. This is the power of knowing your story and using it.

The Superpower Storytelling Framework

Let's first start from the foundations of the framework. The framework relies on two key principles:

- What's at stake for the audience, AND
- Who you are is the most interesting thing about what you do.

When there something at stake, your audience has a reason to care about what happens next. There's real urgency. There's a cost to inaction. Adding this type of pressure to conversation polarizes your audience. Helping them to identify themselves as candidates to join you on your mission.

Further when we add the personal elements of who you are, it helps place authenticity as one of the most important elements in your story.

Stories from your life are the most unique things about you. Offering the biggest potential differentiator in the marketplace. We start from this foundation because it gives us the most to work with.

To further explain, I'll share an analogy.

As you are aware, some well-known brands have headquarters in those tall buildings downtown. Imagine if that big and shiny building had no rooms inside. It stood there, imposing, taking up lots of space but couldn't offer anyone a place to work, live or even to sit. Imagine that it's all a show.

This is what most influencers are like.

They take up a lot of space in the conversation but their branding is hollow; they don't have anything of real depth to offer. There's not much trust in the interaction. They rely on visuals and, once you open the door to interact with them, there's nothing inside.

When we build with story, we build the foundation of why – why we make the choices we make and why people should care. It's a foundation based in truth. Truth about what we've been through to get to where we are – the creation of unbridled authenticity.

You can't outsource authenticity. It's not something that you can fake with a good photographer or colorful branding. Story helps cast a wide foundation, highlighting the truth of what you and your brand are about.

That's how we can begin to get the attention of tenants who plan on moving into those tall buildings. Storytellers are closer to the ground. We can move around better and we can access more people.

We're not stuck in an entrenched environment grasping for substance to prop up our brands. We are ourselves.

That's what the *Superpower Storytelling Framework* will cover. While this framework is simple, it can take some time to get it right. It is my hope that the process will help you to do a little soul-searching and help you to know yourself better.

Once you have the framework down, you'll be ready for almost every storytelling scenario and storytelling will become your newest Superpower.

Whatever your reason for wanting to claim storytelling as your newest Superpower, the goals of this framework are to:

- Give you clarity on the stories that you already have,
- To show you how and where they fit and...
- To give you the structure and confidence to deploy your stories no matter the context.

But before you put on your cape and survey your city from atop a tall building, open your copy of the *Superpower Storytelling Workbook* and let's implement the framework while you learn it.

Storytelling Exercise

Get your *Superpower Storytelling Workbook* here.

Scan the QR Code with your phone!

Your Three Audiences

There are three audiences you will encounter as a member of this human existence, whether we're talking about your life as a business owner or as a citizen of the world. You'll want to manage communication and storytelling for these three groups. Certain story types work better for each group depending on the context you're in.

For sanity's sake, we're gonna boil these down into three specific groups. We'll discuss the types of stories that work best later on in the chapter.

Audience #1:

Think about Audience #1 as any external group you want to influence or do business with.

Here are three:

Group 1: Your Prospects

These are people you speak to on the phone about your products or services – those that you want to help improve in some form or fashion. This includes anyone external to your company in a sales or partnership capacity.

Group 2: Your Investors

If you have investors, you'll need to have the capacity to tell them the appropriate stories. Investors lose attention quickly. Stories get them locked in. Storytelling will win you the capital you need to scale.[28] The ability to conjure up emotions in your investors will give you access to more money. Think Airbnb founders Joe Gebbia, Brian Chesky and Nathan Blecharczyck. During their fundraising journey they gifted a box of "O-bama O's" to investor Paul Graham after he denied them. Upon further questioning, Graham learned that the team funded the company by selling their cereal. He saw something in them and invited them to join Y Combinator. The rest is history.

Group 3: Your Marketing

Marketing is a game of attention. We gain attention for our work through consistency. Stories are a great way to pull people into what you're building and to share why it's important to them. Have you seen the trend of building in public? Boom. This is storytelling at its finest. It takes people along the journey of creation.

Storytelling in your marketing will add clarity for your ideal audience. It will be clear whom you serve, how you can solve their pain, and why it is in their best interest to pay attention.

Audience #2

The second audience is your team. Think of this audience as your co-founders, co-workers or your employees.

These are the people who share space with you inside of your company. You're all striving toward a similar goal or outcome. If you manage a team and are responsible for operating a business, you'll need a unifying thesis. A story in this case is a cause your team can rally behind. You'll want a set of stories to help keep your team focused, motivated and moving in the right direction, regardless of what's happening outside of the organization.

Why is this important?

This can work magic during periods of uncertainty. If your team is unsure of what to do or how their work has an effect on the goals of the company, story can keep them on task and on target.

Audience #3

The third storytelling audience is for when you are public facing. This is talking to people at conferences, guesting on podcasts or speaking from the stage.

Some of you may not speak from the stage right now and may say to yourself: "That's not what I wanna do," and that's fine. You should still possess the necessary skills. You never know. Has anyone ever asked you to address a room of people on short notice? Yep, me too.

Case in point of the soft skill not being so soft anymore. Think of this as how you answer the dreaded question: "So, what do you do?"

You've heard it before. Do you dislike the question as much as I do? You've seen people at conferences come up to you...

Do you want to have a story to tell instead of reciting your name, industry and seniority? If you're reading this book, we'll find it together.

* * * * *

Story is your business card. Business cards are cool, if not a bit outdated. My go-to move at events was to take a photo of a business card and pass it back to the owner. I'm never in the market for more paper to throw away. Traditional business cards are more about exchanging contact information than about being human.

Stories are much more interesting than name, rank and serial number. They also have a side benefit: they make you memorable. Remember humans retain 65%-70% of information when shared in story form.[29]

Think about that for a second. Facts are important but often lack context. Stories leverage values, lessons and steward the transfer of information in a human context.

Stories are an access card into rooms that you're not in. Who doesn't like to tell a juicy story to their friends or colleagues? No one – that's who.

Your stories can become how people tell others about you and your work. Stories are a referral machine. Story is a funnel. Stories build the all-important trust needed to make a sale or to influence others. Equip these three audiences with stories to tell about you.

The Four Questions You Need To Ask Before You Tell A Story

Telling a story is cool. However, telling a story without a purpose is the quickest way to leave an audience confused. No one's gonna get much out of it.

Yeah, it could be an interesting and dramatic story full of flair. Feel free to insert whatever adjective you choose to describe your story. But what's the point of it? To get straight to the point, we must begin with the end in mind.

There are four questions you need to ask before you choose to tell a story. These four questions will guide you in creating the why behind your stories. They highlight which stories to tell so that we can answer how our audience should approach taking action.

So next time you're using a story, regardless of context, make sure you can answer these four questions.

Question 1: What's at Stake For Your Audience?

Ever heard the expression: the stakes are high or high stakes poker?

Those are two common examples to illustrate that something hangs in the balance – that there is something to win or lose. They illustrate that something is at risk. Something hinges on the outcome of what happens next.

In reference to storytelling, it's story element number 2: Conflict. (Described in further detail in Chapter 2 – *The Five Elements of Story*).

When we ask what's at stake, we're answering: What could happen if the audience doesn't pay attention or worse, if they don't take action? Framing the stakes sets the tone for how important taking action is. The stakes paint a picture of the landscape or circumstances in our industry, our lives or for our future. We must have stakes to create the all important FOMO – (fear of missing out) on an opportunity.

Here are a few example questions to frame the stakes in your stories:

For Example

- What sea changes are happening in the industry?
- What is the cost of not taking action?
- What changes are coming that will create a divide in the marketplace?
- Who will win and who will lose?
- Where is the danger?
- What is up for grabs to the victors?
- How likely are these risks to happen?
- Where are your blindspots? What's happening in them right now?

Write down the answers to these questions in your *Superpower Storytelling Workbook*.

Question 2:
What Does Your Audience Want to Learn or Achieve?

Take a second to think through this question: What outcome does your audience want in reference to what's at stake? It's important to understand whom you're speaking with.

We must start with the outcome(s) our audiences want or need to see.

For Example

- How do I win?
- Why do you want a new Superpower?
- Do you feel powerless?
- Do you know that there's something really important that you need to share with the world?
- Is there only one way to do it?
- Do you want to have more confidence when you communicate?
- Did you recently raise capital for your company and now your team is expecting you to lead them?

It's a strength knowing what your audience wants, needs and fears. Label the outcome that will make your audience want to invest their time. Know it and make it easy for them to attach to. Think: how do we articulate that problem?

How do we make sure that whenever someone sees us or our content that they know we understand their pain? When we know what our audience wants to learn or achieve, we can point them toward a specific goal or outcome.

When the audience sees their desired outcome, they're more likely to pay attention. This means we're helping individuals to reconnect with their own stories.

This level of understanding is an essential cog in the wheel of building your tribe of supporters. This is how we find great clientele. Great clients are ambitious. Great clients constantly want to learn and achieve new things.

If you want to change the status quo, knowing what the audience wants to learn or achieve is a differentiating step. It's a relationship builder and giving people what they want is the name of the game.

Does your audience want to achieve better health? Do they want to make more money or are they seeking stronger relationships?

Does your audience want to learn how to make more money? How to save money? How to decrease risk? Or how to increase efficiency in their business?

These are some key questions to ask. That's why *The Magnificent Seven Reasons People Buy* are important for building great stories (as we will discuss in Chapter 5).

Question 3:
How Do You Want Your
Audience to Feel?

Like it or not, we humans are emotional creatures. As emotional creatures, we make emotional decisions. Harvard professor Gerald Zaltman says that 95% of our purchasing decisions take place in the subconscious.[29]

Take a step back and think about that for a second...

That means a paltry 5% of our purchasing decisions take place in our conscious minds. Look around the room you're currently reading this in. 95% of the items in it are results of emotional decisions. This demonstrates our propensity to use emotions to identify what is worthwhile.

Once we've emotionally bought into a decision, then we back into the logic. The tangibility of measurable results, investment cost, likelihood of success, etc.

Now what does that mean for you, your business and your stories?

It's simple:

In sales, the winning ingredients for great businesses are building know, like and trust – as quickly as possible. For the record, sales here isn't only revenue generation. It can mean getting buy-in from stakeholders in your company or winning a discount at the local coffee shop. Sales is getting someone on your team and driving the scenario toward a mutually beneficial outcome.

Stories are a great way to build know, like and trust. When people know you, they can like you. After they like you, it's easier for them to trust you. Building trust means you've crossed the emotional barrier with your buyer. You've demonstrated understanding of how they feel right now with their problem.

Help them to identify with the message you're sharing to the world. Let's look at some example phrases that conjure emotion in an audience:

- Imagine
- Have you ever?
- When was the last time that you...

Phrases like these create resonance with the individual's emotions from their own context. Labeling the emotions you want your audience to feel is the first step to knowing which stories to share. Sharing a point of conflict in your stories will help your audience arrive at an emotion they can't hide from.

This is the unknown, unsaid problem (see Chapter 5). Agitate that problem by creating an emotional space. They'll feel fear, pride, excitement or think that they've almost got it all figured out. But throughout stories they'll learn that they're missing a few crucial steps.

Leveraging these emotions will help your audience to see themselves in your stories. Making it easier for you to get your audiences in the right emotional state to receive your message.

To kick it up a notch – fold in the remaining 5% with logic.

Our species is quite advanced with technology. We've built some incredible things. We can communicate across the world in an instant, send payments at the blink of an eye with crypto currency, and we can fly to nearly anywhere in the world in about a day by airplane.

However, no matter how advanced our technology becomes, we're still humans at the end of the day, at least for now (we'll see what happens after Elon Musk's *Neuralink*).

Which means we're going to make decisions on an emotional level before we do anything else. It's our job as leaders to create that emotion.

Emotional decision-making means getting our audience involved in their own story. That way they can see exactly how we're part of the same tribe. I use the terms "customer" and "audience" interchangeably. So your customers could be your team, folks you mentor, or it could be people you speak to from the stage. Insert whichever context works for your situation.

As storytellers, our job is to take the audience through an emotional ride that creates a gap in their minds. A gap we can help you fill with our products, services and solutions.

Question 4:
What Do You Want the Audience to Do Next?

This is the place where I see most people fumble with storytelling.

Lots of people have great stories. They've got everyone in the room eating out of the palm of their hand. The crowd firmly on their side. People are coming up to them after a speech, visiting the website. Sometimes they even win a client or two but couldn't tell you what, why or how it happened.

Here's why: there was no clear call to action. The audience doesn't know what to do next. Things changed significantly once I realized this. When using a story to label your audience's pain, build a gap between where they are and where they want to go.

Telling your audience what to do next is calling them to action. We need to label what we want the audience to do before we start telling stories. They're listening to us and we're able to help them see themselves in the action of the story. Now we are their guide. We've shown them the path to their own hero's journey and now it's our chance to tell them how to get started.

For your quiver, here are a few examples of telling the audience what to do next:

- Download a lead magnet.
- Join the course.

- Get a copy of my book.

- Get on a free call with your team.

- Come to Monday's team meeting with five ideas as to how we can improve the company.

- Download the latest podcast episode and subscribe.

- Go outside and bury your head in the sand for 25 minutes and meditate.

- Start your diet transformation journey.

- Text me at XYZ what resonated most from this episode.

- Head over to Amazon and leave a review of *Superpower Storytelling* – seriously, you can do it right here, right now :).

Scan the QR Code with your phone!

Whatever the call to action is, we need to label it and make it clear to our audience. Asking this question before you start storytelling gives you control over the outcome. Oh, yeah, and make a single call to action per situation. Don't confuse your audience with too many options. Confused people don't buy anything.

Let's go over a few examples of well-placed CTA's that you can use as inspiration in your next piece of content, speech or podcast.

Podcast/ Keynote Lead Magnet CTAs

- If you're looking for clarity on whether your business is at risk for XYZ, then take your phone and scan this QR code.

- You can download our assessment. It will show exactly where your business is at risk {Insert Metric or topic}.

- After you've taken the assessment, if you score a six or lower, we should talk.

- If you want to talk further about solving these challenges, we can hop on a call.

Podcast Download CTAs

- For those listening, head over to {Insert website Link}. You can get the latest guide and learn how to {INSERT BENEFIT}. See you there!

- Want to {achieve X}? Use the code {XYZ} to get 10% off your first order.

- To hear more about how we {achieved XYZ result}, subscribe to the podcast and check out Episode 25 for the step-by-step breakdown.

Social Media Posts CTAs

- Comment the word {INSERT Word} below if you'd like a copy of the guide/ if this post resonates with you.

- What do you think? Comment Below!

- Tag someone who {insert Value prop}.

A call to action might be the most important thing that you have in any story you tell. This goes for any speech, podcast conversation, or across your marketing channels. Our job as storytellers is to guide people toward their next step – to guide them to take action.

Make it crystal clear what you want done and why your audience will benefit. Psst – the call to action has to do with what your audience wants to learn or achieve.

If you tie these four questions together before you choose which stories to tell, you're locked in. You're locked in on why you're telling the story, what it's gonna do for the audience and why listening to you is worth it.

And if you can tell them what to do next to start solving their problem, you've got them started on the story as the protagonist. They're the hero and you are the guide. Now it's all about helping them complete their part of the story.

Now let's go over the three stories you need to lead.

The Three Stories You Need To Lead

In life, each of us has our own unique history, friendships, adversities and triumphs. Each of us experiences many different life-changing events over the course of our lifetime – events that shape who we are.

Perhaps you built a successful business in your youth. Or you lost someone important in your family at a crucial time. Or a special person changed the way you define purpose in your life. There may not be one singular event that stands out to you – but don't worry. We'll get there.

The moments we notice depend on the context.

Nothing resonates more with an audience than when you are your actual authentic self. And the way you can do that is by telling your own stories. All the moments or experiences that happened to you and only to you. You know the lessons from these events and only you can access them in your mind's eye.

When you share your stories, it allows you to come to the forefront of what you do. Who you are is the most interesting thing about what you do. That needs to become an important part of what you are telling people.

The clearer we are about that, the easier it is for us to strike a chord with whomever we want to serve. Through my research, I found that there are three types of stories that each of us already has.

Three types of stories that are closely related but slightly different. These three types of stories are ones that you can find from your own life. With these stories, you'll be able to access parts of your story and understand the why behind what you do.

When you understand the why behind what you do, you have the ability to help others understand and attach to it too. The best part?

No one in your market – even if you're in a crowded one – can leverage your unique stories. If they ever tried to, it would come off as being fake. With that said, there are three types of stories that you already have from your life and your business.

You can use them whether writing for social media, a keynote speech, or speaking on a podcast.

Storytelling Exercise

Open up your *Superpower Storytelling Workbook* and Get your workbook here:

Scan the QR Code with your phone!

The workbook will help you organize your stories and outline the best context to use them. The exercise will give you clarity and confidence to deploy stories in any context.

Don't worry, we'll cover a few examples so you can get a clear idea of each one.

Let's jump into the three stories you already have.

1) Mission/ Origin Story

The mission.

Stories of our mission are our origin stories. They outline your purpose. What you do and how you do it. It's a guide-post keeping you locked in on the day to day.

Think about any of your unique personality traits. What was the first time that you became aware that you had this particular trait?

Were you a child on the playground and you showed stubbornness by refusing to leave? Does your family always talk about one of your specific stories? Do you have a nickname? How did you get it?

Another example might be: what was the moment you knew that you had to do the work that you're doing now? When did you know you had to start this company?

When did you know that you had to quit your job and go do something different?

What was the decisive moment? What was the emotion you experienced when you decided to take the future into your own hands?

Diving further, we can think about your career. Did you have mentors or circumstances that pushed you into doing what you do now?

Did you create your company, service or product to help your past self? (For example, you didn't have the help you needed when you were getting started, so you created your product or service to solve this problem for others.)

Where'd you get started? What was the movement you knew that you had to share this message with the world?

Here are a few examples:

Superman

- From the last ship off of Krypton.
- Lands on earth.
- Clark Kent discovers his powers but doesn't know what to do with them.
- Clark Kent becomes a reporter, sees all the crime and corruption in Metropolis and decides to do something about it.
- He starts fighting crime and begins his work to save the world.

Steve Jobs At Apple

Steve Jobs was notoriously brash, direct, and had a wild vision for what computers could do for humankind. Apple employees have varying viewpoints on his working style.

Though during Job's time at the helm of Apple, he was able to galvanize the company. Pushing employees and their boundaries well beyond what they thought possible.

His mission statement proves it:

> *"To make a contribution to the world by making tools for the mind that advance humankind."*[30]

Think about the story that Mission statement tells to employees, contractors and vendors. It screams that their efforts are going toward something MUCH greater than themselves. This is a cause that makes it easy to rally the troops to dig deeper.

Elon Musk With Tesla And SpaceX

The controversial entrepreneur is on multiple seemingly impossible missions.

Musk spearheads a shift to electric cars, reusable rocketry, and boring tunnels below congested cites to help with traffic and the hopeful mission to Mars.

Musk's successes are incredible advancements for humankind. They draw the ire of critics and inspire many. Musk powers these seemingly impossible pursuits with his personal mission:

> *"If something is important enough, you should try, even if the probable outcome is failure."* [28]

This approach has made him one of the richest man in the world at the time of this writing. Between these two companies, he employs tens of thousands of people who help in the pursuit of advancing humankind.

Oprah Winfrey And Harpo

You're no doubt familiar with Oprah Winfrey's media empire. Oprah came from humble beginnings as a TV correspondent in Nashville, Tennessee.[31]

In the 1980's, the Oprah Winfrey Show became the highest-rated talk show in television history, which secured her meteoric rise. Over her career, she's inspired and educated millions of people all over the world.

Her influence and charisma spawned a network and a magazine that exemplify her mission:

> *"To be a teacher. And to be known for inspiring my students to be more than they thought they could be."*[32]

It's clear that Oprah has made good on her mission – leading many to go beyond what they thought they could.

Lots of people want to be part of these missions. The products and services provided by these leaders and their companies' impact our lives every day.

2) Vision/ Success/ Aspirations

Vision outlines your long-term aspirations. It's a communication of desired outcomes. It's meant to inspire and motivate audiences. In essence, what do YOU want to achieve? When you think about stories and vision, think about what you want to achieve in the long term. The larger and more specific your vision is, the larger the audience you can build around it.

Think of your vision in two ways:

1. What you want to see take place in the world. This is what happens when your mission is complete.

2. A guidepost for your team and/or your family.

Your vision is your thesis. Every business needs one. A thesis is a guide to keep your business on track and to keep your employees engaged. Your vision is a cause your team can rally behind at all times.

For example:

Corporate branding is all about creating a consistent brand image. Corporate branding differs from product branding. With product branding the goal is to distinguish a single product. Corporate branding is about creating culture.

To carry this through, corporations need to start with their own employees.

Communicating the values of a brand is the first step to presenting a brand to the public.[33] People want to work for an exciting, fast growing company. A story they can be a part of. Big visions draw big crowds.

Do you want to work with 10,000 entrepreneurs to help them become the best version of themselves? Do you want to combat climate change or child trafficking?

What is your vision? Take a moment and write down what you want the world to look like in the future. There are no wrong answers here. View this through the lens of your skillset, mindset and the people you want to affect. Vision works well for a business brand as well as for an individual brand.

Here are a few examples of vision stories:

Brian Chesky – Co-Founder, Airbnb

I remember the first time I stayed in an Airbnb.

My brothers and I took a trip to Bangkok, Thailand. I registered for the website and within 15 minutes, I had a stay booked. I thought was the coolest thing to book someone's apartment on the other side of the world. Millions of others agreed.

Airbnb has facilitated over 393.7 million bookings since 2007. They've generated over $63.21 billion in booking value revenue worldwide.[34]

Their success enabled the team to take their company public in 2020.

The guiding principle of co-founder Brian Chesky's vision encapsulates what Airbnb is about.

"To create a world where anyone can belong anywhere."[35]

Larry Page And Sergey Brin, Alphabet (Google) Co-Founders

Back in the 1990s – if you can remember that long ago – the internet was a nascent place full of untapped potential.

Newsweek magazine disagreed declaring, "No online database will ever replace your daily newspaper."[36]

Oh how wrong they were.

Where pundits saw a fad, a pair of PhD students at Stanford University saw opportunity.

Larry Page and Sergay Brin decided to explore the mathematical properties of the web.

Things escalated quickly.

And not six years later the company was pulling in $2.7 billion in annual revenue. Google IPO'd at valuation of $23 billion – an insane amount for a six-year-old company. [37] [38]

While their methods and mission have changed, their vision is still running strong:

> *"To organize the world's information and make it universally accessible and useful."*[39]

Mary Kay Ash, Founder Of Mary Kay Cosmetics [37]

In the fall of 1963, Mary Kathlyn Wagner, retired from her position at Stanley Home Products. Wagner left after the executive team passed on promoting her in favor of one of her male trainees.

She intended to use her retirement to write a book helping women to go further in business. As fate would have it, that book turned into the business plan for Mary's ideal company. That company became Mary Kay Cosmetics.

Wagner put her skills from a 20+ year career at Stanley Home Products to set up her first store in Dallas, Texas, called "Beauty by Mary Kay." She employed nine sales women.[40]

By 1964, Wagner changed her name to Mary Kay Ash and the company blossomed growing by double digits every year.

Mary began providing business education seminars for women. And started Mary Kay's annual tradition of recognizing top women entrepreneurs.

"At Mary Kay, you are in business for yourself, but not by yourself. God didn't have time to make a nobody. As a result, you can have, or be, anything you want."[21]

Even though Mary has passed on, the company that bears her name holds up the mantle to her vision. In 1996, Forbes called Mary Kay Ash one of their greatest business stories of all time. Today, Mary Kay cosmetics employs over three million consultants worldwide. The business achieves a wholesale volume of more than three billion units.

And rounding out the three stories you need to lead, we head over to milestones.

Milestones

Milestones are stories each of us has.

They are those moments of adversity. The best part? No one can compete with us on our milestone stories.

How you ask? Think about this:

Imagine that the both of us:

Grew up in the same town, on the same street, attended the same high school and college where were both rowed crew. After college we both moved back to our hometown, and started careers in the exact same sector. Our life experiences, while similar, will have completely different inflection points.

Which means, we'll never be in competition for who we are. The competition happens for what we do. Many people offer products and services like we do.

While they work with the same types of clients and charge similar prices, they can't compete with who we are. Which is why it's important – especially in these times – to start investing in your story.

Your story will differentiate you in the marketplace. Allowing YOUR people to see you differently from everyone else in your field. That's the importance of storytelling in business.

Our stories are unique to our lives, to our experience and to our point of view. Thus, our stories are some of the coolest and most interesting things about us. Especially stories about adversity or challenges that we've experienced along the way.

These are the moments that show agency over circumstances. The true measure of the human spirit. What are some of the most challenging experiences from your life? Did you grow up in extreme poverty or did you grow up without your parents?

Did you eventually find someone who encouraged you to go to college or gave you your first job? To build your company? Perhaps you got divorced and lost everything and you bounced back.

Maybe you had to start over but in five short years, you're back and better than ever financially and mentally. Maybe you had massive student loans and you were able to pay them off. You can share how you've overcome challenges.

What lesson did you learn from doing that work? What emotions come to mind? Milestones stories are great because they create a natural emotional arc essential to great storytelling. You've experienced something tough and now you're on to something better.

Milestone stories can also come from your customers. They can speak to the before and after of the results you helped them achieve. You're showing that you can turn less than favorable circumstances into something positive.

Here's are some examples:

Hal Elrod, Author Of The Miracle Morning

Hal Elrod literally died at the age 20 in a head-on collision caused by a drunk driver. His heart stopping for a full six minutes. If that weren't enough, the car wreck broke eleven of his bones and had him in a coma for six whole days. Hal survived all of that only to wake up and have doctors tell him that he'd likely never walk again.

Hal set his sights on making a full recovery and, through hard work, diligence and owning the morning; he became an ultra-marathoner before his 30th birthday.

It doesn't stop there though. In November of 2016, Hal was diagnosed with a rare and aggressive form of leukemia that attacked his kidneys, lungs and heart. With death knocking on his door once again, Hal set himself on a mission to:

"Elevate the consciousness of humanity, one morning and one person at a time."[21]

His leukemia is in remission and Hal tours the world helping people to see their potential and transform their lives.

You can see the many inflection points in Hal's journey that show the incisive moments that started him on his mission.

Business Coach Example

You are a business coach. You have an all-star customer. They weren't an all-star when you first started working together. Matter of fact, their company was in dire straits.

Their business was stagnant and they were in one of the darkest times in their lives. Lead volume was down and employee morale was at an all-time low. And when your client signed up to work with you, they hadn't won any revenue in the last six months. The client wasn't sure what to do next.

They came to you for help. Using your coaching method, you were able to pinpoint the problem in the business. And reframe the mindset of the founder in the process. Within six months, you were able to get the business to its highest earning month ever.

The best part?

Your system will allow them to make repeatable results going forward.

Insert your own version of creating results for a client if you're using this type of story for your business.

Milestone stories show that you have experience helping people get past big problems. And they allow your audience to see themselves achieving similar results. Milestone stories create emotional bonds through their demonstration of agency over a problem or circumstance.

It says to the subconscious: there are results on the other side of our work together.

Here are a few guided questions to ask yourself as you go through the exercises in the workbook:

- Where have you experienced adversity in your life or in your business?
- What are some of the MOST challenging experiences you've been through in your life?
- How did they make you feel?
- What are you doing now?
- How did you overcome the adversity?
- What did you learn from the adversity?
- How did you apply it? How can others apply it?

A Personal Milestone Example

Like you, I have a few milestone stories of my own. Over my career I've collected experiences that have profoundly changed how I approach life and business.

I'm sure that more are coming as well.

But one milestone story stands out for me. It's a moment that shaped my stance on personal accountability. It gave me a keen understanding that no one is coming to save me.

It took me years to get up enough courage to share the story. After a lot of encouragement from my mentors, I finally shared the story when a prospect asked me why I chose to be an entrepreneur.

The story landed immediately. I closed a deal on account of it.

Remember, you can share your vulnerabilities while sharing important lessons. They're the context that makes you the best fit for your prospects.

Here's my milestone:

The Barback

Let's take it back to 2010 – during the last global recession.

I was 22 years old. I was six months out of college. Living with my parents out in Queens, New York. I was sleeping in my childhood twin bed. My feet dangled off the edges even diagonally because I'm too tall.

I'd applied for over 300 jobs in those six months – hadn't gotten a single interview and no offers. I had $2.96 in my bank account, $60k+ in student debt and I had my first student loan payment due in a few weeks.

Something had to give.

I knew that waiting for responses was taking too long. So, after much self-talk in the mirror, I decided that I'd better go walking around and look for a job at a restaurant or a bar to get some cash in the door.

I was tremendously scared of doing this, almost on the verge of throwing up. ME, a college-educated person having to humble himself and go door to door to ask for a minimum wage job? What part of the game is this??

I walked into ten places a day for a week and by the weekend I had a job offer to be a barback. Not glamorous, But it was a place to start.

It was a Sunday evening.

I was working at The Charleston, a dive bar on N. 7th/Bedford Ave. in Williamsburg Brooklyn. Back then they had a Cajun restaurant that made southern comfort food, po'boys and the like. The most popular drink – a shot of Evan Williams and a Miller High Life. Classy.

I was 8:34pm – the beginning of my eight-hour shift and I was about to experience one of the lowest points in my life.

Part of my glamorous job included taking out the trash. I squeezed myself past the restaurant's 55-gallon drum of spent fryer oil in the alleyway so I could get to the trash bins. I worked quickly and methodically. In no time I was finally on my last bag of trash.

The last bag though, was stuck DEEP in the can as if Oscar The Grouch himself was holding tightly to its prized contents. I pulled and pulled. Nothing.

Gritting my teeth, I squatted down to work the bag free. With a fervent and persistent tug, the bag dislodged.

VICTORY!

I thought, cursing the bag.

Suddenly, I was consumed with abject fear as a 1.75 liter bottle of liquor in the trash bag clipped the edge of the oil barrel at the absolute perfect angle; so perfect, in fact, that it caused the barrel to wobble and the lid to pop off.

The barrel started to lean. My breathing stopped.

The sound of trash bag dripping on my foot, fell away.

A full body heat appeared – you know the kind you have when you know you've messed up big?

BOOM!

I was covered in cold fryer oil, fryer shake, and shrimp crumbs. And the spill was spreading quickly inside the bar toward the basement.

Dropping the trash bag, I ran inside and attempted to stop the spill with my shoes, my sweatshirt... a broom – anything.

No dice. I had two options:

- Tell Dorian, the bartender that I quit and that this is the last time he'd see me, or

- Suck it up and clean up the spill like nothing happened hoping he wouldn't fire me.

Wiping the oil off of my forehead with my clean forearm, it hit me.

I can't quit. It hit me: I don't have anywhere else to go. It hit me: I don't have anyone I can call. It hit me: I have a student loan payment due the following week and need this job to pay for it.

I had absolutely, positively. Nothing.

I was speechless.

I was overcome with the perfect mix of anger, sadness and powerlessness. The kind that you keep close to you. The kind you realize that it's better to never forget. The kind that either breaks you or becomes your first building block.

Then out of nowhere, a third option hit me. Finish the night. And use this moment.

I didn't know how. I didn't know what. But I knew that no matter what it took... I was going to have something. I'd win somehow and that this moment would be the first brick in my wall of ambition.

I worked six more months in the bar, networked my face off and landed a job at a construction company. And my story really began.

Keep the hard times close.

The question is, what is YOUR oil spill?

Storytelling Exercise

So here's how we're gonna do this. First things firsts (I Poppa) open up your *Superpower Storytelling Workbook*.

Get it here:

Scan the QR Code with your phone!

Open up to the "Story Purge" exercise and let's configure which one of these stories has the most emotional depth.

Once you've completed the exercise jump back in here.

* * * * *

Welcome back! Which story resonated with you the most?

When you think about it, you say to yourself: this was a decisive moment in my life or my career.

Let's grab that one and start to unpack it.

Let's see what's important about it.

- Who are the important characters?
- Is it you?
- Your best friend, your family members, a client?

- What is the plot?

- What's actually happening inside of the story?

- What is conflict?

- Where is the incisive moment where things change?

- What does that look like?

- What does that feel like?

- Where does the story take place? Is that important?

- Why is it important to you?

- What is the theme or lesson you want people to take from the story and apply to their own lives?

One of the most important elements of story is showing our agency over stress or circumstances. Stories of conflict are incredible tools for demonstrating the human experience.

Each of us will experience hardship in our lives. Some ideas to draw from:

- Were you bullied as a kid?

- Did you lose your business?

- Did you go through a divorce?

- Something tough happened to you but you didn't quit?

The fact that you're still here is a clear representation of what is actually important in the story. Overcoming challenges shows your audience that they too can overcome. Taking people back to a challenge humanizes you and your business. As long as we humanize what we do, who we are and the why behind it, we're set up to win.

Take a few minutes to review the stories from your life and organize them into the categories we outlined in the chapter, you'll see a few clear winning stories that you can start to leverage in your business.

Now let's take these stories and make them crisp and refreshing.

CHAPTER 4

Crisping Your Content

"If you want to get ahead, focus on your communication skills. That's because what's really essential is being able to get others to follow your ideas. If you're a salesperson, you want people to follow your advice. If you're a management leader, you want them to follow you in business. If you can't communicate, it's like winking at a girl in the dark – nothing happens. You can have all the brainpower in the world, but you have to be able to transmit it. And the transmission is communication."

Warren Buffett

Would you agree that the capacity to turn your ideas into crisp statements that move people to swift and decisive action is a valuable skill in business? I would too.

If Warren Buffet, the "Oracle of Omaha," says that focusing on your communication is an essential skill if you want people to follow you or your advice, then that's good enough for me.

Your most important sales tools are the words that come out of your mouth. This applies whether you're selling insurance, raising funds or rallying your team.

Regardless of what you're selling, you're going to need to create buy-in.

The way you articulate your point of view and your ability to command your words are the fastest ways to build trust. If you can tell stories and deliver those stories in a confident manner, you're ahead of the competition.

What's that you say? You're not selling? If you want to convince your executive team to go with your proposal over other options – you are selling. If you're at an event recruiting quality talent to join your company – you're selling. If you're creating social media posts, videos, and leveraging marketing channels... you guessed it. You're selling.

You're selling whether you admit it or not. If you're going to sell, you might as well sell with strength, confidence and conviction – right?

In this chapter, we're going to cover two frameworks that will help you to develop stronger methods of communication of your stories and ideas: The A.R.E.A Framework – a delivery method to help you speak in soundbites and sound like an expert every time you speak – and The P.E.A.R. Method – a purpose-built method to captivate your audiences and bring them into your stories, in order to deliver presentations, workshops and podcast interviews for massive engagement.

Let's paint a quick picture:

You're prepared for that podcast or keynote. You did your research, practiced in front of the mirror and you're ready to be the most interesting person in the room. The host even sent you questions in advance so you're feeling relaxed and prepared.

The podcast is going great. You're building a real rapport with the host and you know the authentic you is peeking out. It's a wonderful feeling. Then the unimaginable happens... The host asks you a question that wasn't on the prep list. You're not prepared....

What now?

The whole recording was going so well...

This question could ruin everything...

You might not sound like an expert anymore...

Fret not, that's what the A.R.E.A. framework is built for.

The A.R.E.A. Framework

Powerful storytelling has clear structure. Stories have arcs. Ups and downs. Reasons, emotions and evidence. These are the tools of the trade. They can carry your audience through an arc allowing them to feel, be heard, and understood.

I found the A.R.E.A Framework to be the simplest way to help me organize speeches, workshops, and sales call scripts. If I get thrown a curveball question and have to respond on the fly, I answer with this framework. It gives me a chance to slow down, to think and to form my opinion while I respond. My personal favorite use of the framework, though, is handling sales objections. It'll help you communicate with authority and thoroughness.

Below you'll find examples of how to use The A.R.E.A. Framework:

A

Let's start with the letter A.

The A in A.R.E.A stands for Angle.

For any topic or question that you get, first come up with your angle or viewpoint on the topic.

What is your opinion on the topic or situation? What do you believe to be true? What position are you defending? State that.

Let's pretend that you're on a podcast and the host asks:

> *"Electric cars are growing in popularity... are they more efficient than non-electric cars?"*

Using the A.R.E.A. Framework, you would state your opinion. For our example, we're going to give you the position of liking electric cars.

You'd say something like:

> *A = "Electric cars are more efficient and better for the environment than non-electric cars."*

That is our angle. We're going to defend this position as we walk through the rest of the A.R.E.A Framework.

Now let's move on to the next letter.

R

The R in A.R.E.A. stands for Reason.

Now that you have an angle, to sound like an expert you must provide a cause or reason for holding your point of view.

Having a point of view is cool, but experts have reason and thought behind their viewpoints.

In the case of electric cars, if they are more efficient than non-electric cars, we want to state the reason that they are.

To kick off reasoning through our position phrases like "The reason is..." or "That's because..." work well.

For example:

> A: *"Electric cars are more efficient and better for the environment than non-electric cars."*

> R: *"The reason electric cars are more efficient is because they don't emit greenhouse gasses."*

Let's keep building on this example. Yep, we're going to enhance your position as an eclectic car expert.

Didn't think you were going to be one when you started this exercise, huh?

No worries – that's what the A.R.E.A. Framework can do!

Onward to letter E.

E

The next part of the framework is the letter E.

E stands for Evidence.

So far we have our angle on and we've provided a reason for our point of view. Now it's time to flex our expertise and provide evidence for our claim. Use evidence to enrich your angle.

Evidence will show that you've done your homework and that you understand what you're talking about.

To kick off the evidence portion of our position, a phrase like, "For example..." works well.

Your three story types will also fit well here to provide evidence and examples for any position you take.

To keep the electric car example going we would say:

A: *"Electric cars are more efficient and better for the environment than non-electric cars."*

R: *"The reason electric cars are more efficient is because they don't emit greenhouse gasses."*

E: *"For Example, across the industry, gasoline-powered engines are 25 to 30% efficient, but less so when compared to electric motors, which are about 90% efficient."*[42]

A

The final letter of the A.R.E.A Framework is one you've seen before. It's the letter A. It's back with a vengeance to close out our message:

The letter A appears to us again as a repeat of our earlier definition: Angle.

We've given our angle, stated our reasons and provided evidence. Now it's time to close it out by restating our angle.

Now we have an evidence sandwich. We have a clear framework to share our opinions, and communicate succinctly – even on the fly.

To kick off a closing out of our position a phrase like "And that's why..." works well.

Like this:

> A: *"Electric cars are more efficient and better for the environment than non-electric cars."*
>
> R: *"The reason electric cars are more efficient is because they don't emit greenhouse gasses."*
>
> E: *"For example, across the industry gasoline-powered engines are 25 to 30% efficient, but less so when compared to electric motors, which are about 90% efficient."*
>
> A: *"And that's why I believe electric cars are more efficient and better for the environment than non- electric cars."*

(For "example prompts" to practice the A.R.E.A. Framework, open your *Superpower Storytelling Workbook*

Scan the QR Code with your phone!

The A.R.E.A. Framework is purpose-built to provide clarity and structure to any argument or opinion that you have. You can use it in your next meeting, on a podcast interview or on your next sales call. Leverage the A.R.E.A. Framework every day to sound like the expert you were born to be.

As I mentioned earlier in this chapter, one of my favorite uses of the A.R.E.A. Framework is using it to handle objections. Handling objections comes up in sales, in the office and in life.

Using the A.R.E.A. Framework is a great way to prepare ourselves for all possible objections. It also gives us a tidy way to plug in our stories.

Our personal stories will fit into the reason and evidence categories with ease.

We can take the A.R.E.A. Framework and smash objections in a clear, concise and repeatable way. Reasons are how you state your product or service works. Evidence is how you prove its worth.

Let's start off with the basics.

Objection Handling With The A.R.E.A. Framework

There are three types of objections we encounter in a sales context. Objections are all some version of:

- "This is too expensive!" Think of that as the price objection.

- "Is this going to work for me?" Also known as the is-this-the-right-solution objection and,

- "Is now the right time?" That means they have a current solution in place or aren't in budget season, etc.

You may field an objection with different wording but generally objections fall into one of these three categories. And that means we should have stories ready to handle these objections.

After all what is an objection really? It's a request for more information. This is where you provide information contrary to the perceived doubt shown in the objection.

For evidence, we can plug in one of these three core story types: Mission, Vision or Milestones. Use whichever story type fits the occasion as an anecdote to counter the objection. Countering objections in this way gives color, evidence and social proof to any claim.

Here are a few examples:

"It's Too Expensive!"

The first and perhaps most important note about a price objection is that price is only an issue if value is a question. If someone isn't prepared to invest in your products or services, then you haven't unlocked the pain associated with where they currently are or with inaction. This 100% means that early in our sales process, we didn't qualify the opportunity well enough. Solid qualification early in the sale makes all the difference.

Head here if you you'd like to learn more about how to properly qualify your prospects over the phone.

Scan the QR Code with your phone!

Think through this for your product or service and, whenever possible, have story examples to help your prospects understand what could happen if they don't take action.

Using the A.R.E.A. Framework, to counter a price objection of, "It's too expensive," we would approach it in the following way:

We'd use a client Milestone story:

> A: I understand your concerns here. The price is actually a great value.

> R: The reason is, one of our best clients had the same concern before she signed up with us.

> E: She's in a similar field as you and works with clients globally. Using our Frameworks, she got her investment back in six weeks of working with us and is on the way to getting a 5x ROI.

> A: And that's why our price is well-valued for someone in your position.

This is how we use a milestone story to show that we've achieved great results for our clients and build confidence in our prospects that we can do the same for them.

"Is This Going To Work For Me?"

Mission stories work well here:

> A: *Based on what I've heard from you so far, a service like this would work really well for you.*
>
> R: *The reason is, that's exactly why we built this company. Our goal is to make it easy for consultants to grow their business while focusing on what they do best – consulting.*
>
> E: *For example, when I started out in my career as a consultant, I had no idea how to get clients. When I'd speak to other consultants just like you, I noticed how persistent of a problem this was. In the last two years, we've worked with over 50 consultants and helped them hit their first six-figures in earnings while working less.*
>
> A: *And that's why, If you want to get back to working on the business and not in the business, this program will work wonders for you.*

Using a Mission Story in this way humanizes you – the seller – by showing parity with your client's pain. You've been there before and experienced the same pain and frustration. This creates feelings of "I'm not alone."

"I Don't Know If Now Is The Right Time"

Vision stories work well for this objection:

> A: *It's actually a great time to get started.*

R: *The reason is, we've engineered this system specifically to accelerate quick wins. Each of our new clients receives a step-by-step action plan and the sooner the plan is set up, the faster we can get you to your goals.*

E: *For example, we've done the math and clients start to see results within three weeks of getting started. They find that it frees up much more time in their business. Clients who wait, often stay in the confused state and wind up spending more time and resources. We want to build a world where every consultant can build a seven-figure business while focusing on what they do best.*

A: *That's why it's actually a great time to get started.*

Vision stories work well to future pace. Future pacing is painting a picture of what things can look like by demonstrating a future state they can expect.

That's how we use the A.R.E.A. Framework to handle objections.

Now that we know the three types of stories you have, and A.R.E.A. Framework. If we want to kick it up a notch, we can use The P.E.A.R. Method to make your stories lush and your presentations sing.

The P.E.A.R. Method

First, let's dive into a Pear – the fruit, that is.

Think of a Bartlett pear. It's juicy. Soft, but not too hard. It fits nicely in the palm of your hand. It's either smooth or coarse like worn sandpaper.

When you pierce the skin of a pear on the first bite, the texture of the pulp hits the palate before a wave of sweetness. The whole palate activates. Each bite is a new discovery until only the husk remains, its role dutifully served.

If it's a hot summer day, it may in fact be time for a second pear. Stories are all about how we take uninteresting moments – like eating a pear – and turn them into something juicy.

Something that keeps the audience salivating for more. If you've ever struggled with how to tell stories that captivate and keep your audience locked in...

Then you're gonna love this technique. It's my go-to technique for workshops, crafting keynotes and enthralling dinner conversation and while performing standup comedy.

This is best suited for presentations, interviews and if you're at a cocktail party being the most interesting person in the room. Telling stories is tough. But keeping an audience on the edge of their seat wanting more? This is next level storytelling.

Will you become a storyteller like David Sedaris after learning this technique?

Who knows... but you will notice some changes. Changes that provide an increase in an audience's attention, and a decrease in people playing on their phones.

Not only is it an acronym but it serves an extra purpose.

The key to The P.E.A.R. Method is that you activate the posterior parietal cortex in your audience. The posterior parietal cortex is the area of the brain responsible for visual working memory and attention.

You're gonna want to activate this area whenever you tell a story. If you want to be memorable, that is ;).

Okay, let's get started with the letter P.

P

The P in P.E.A.R. stands for Present.

Meaning that whenever possible, you should tell every story in the present tense. Many great storytellers, writers and philosophers have come before us. The most engaging ones? They pull us right into the moment. But before we go any further...

I want you to know that this doesn't mean you should copy their stories or the way they deliver them. This means you should take the STORY you're telling and deliver it as if it's happening right then and there. So how do we go about telling a story in the present tense?

Here's a short list for you: Use phrases like "I am," and "It is," instead of saying "I was," or "It was." Think of that moment like a movie playing out in front of you. Speaking in the present tense allows the audience to share that moment with you – in real time.

It also affords you, the orator, the chance to relive your story in that singular moment. Almost like it's happening to you all over again. Your authenticity and creativity can shine through.

You're creating a unique moment between you and your audience. Is this easy? No. It takes a lot of practice. When you've got it down, you'll notice a difference in the way your audience pays attention.

Now let's jump into the letter "E" and dive deeper into how to take the present tense to the next level to lock in your audience.

E

The E in The P.E.A.R. Method stands for Emotion.

This is one of my all-time favorite tactics to use to get your audience on the edge of their seats. The technique works well – in person or virtually. Emotion is the currency of decision making. Telling your audience what you're doing and how you're feeling – in the present tense.

Emotions – also in the present tense – prime your audience for connection. They know how they're supposed to feel too.

For example if I say:

> "It's 2018, and I'm riding my bicycle through Central Park in NYC. A dog runs right out in front of me on the bike path. I'm frightened for the pup as I swerve to avoid it... Unfortunately, I swerve into a group of oncoming cyclists. Over the handlebars I go. Six other bikers also go over the handlebars. I pop up embarrassed – trying to pretend like nothing happened..."

Great storytellers know how to bring emotion into the fold and take the audience along for the ride (no pun intended here with the bike reference, I promise).

By labeling the emotions in your story, you can deepen your connection with the audience.

Okay. Now we're going to talk about the letter A.

A

The A in P.E.A.R. stands for Atmosphere.

There are a couple of different styles of Atmosphere you can add to your stories. Of all the devices in The P.E.A.R. Method, Atmosphere enables you to activate that posterior parietal cortex. (It's the area of the brain responsible for visual working memory and attention, remember?)

Here's how:

Sounds

What does the room, space or situation you're in sound like? What are the sounds of the moment? Does the floor creak? Are the leaves rustling? Are you shoes squeaking on the dew sitting on the grass? Tell us about the sounds.

Take us there with you.

Textures

Describe the room. Is there paint peeling? Is the room covered in wainscoting? Describe it to us! Help us visualize where you are and be in that exact same moment with you.

Smells

Of the five senses gifted to humans, our sense of smell has the deepest link to our memory. Eliciting a smell memory from your audiences locks them into a memory of their own from a similar smell.

What does the room smell like? Are there fresh-baked cookies in the oven? Is the salt of the ocean air wafting in the breeze? Is there a fire roasting in a hearth? I bet you can smell each of them simply by reading the phrases.;)

Sights

When you're in the middle of the action of your story, what do you see? What are you wearing? What colors are in the room? Is there light flickering? Is there a sea of people? Describe what you're seeing with as much relevant detail as you can. The picture will appear in their minds as well.

Example:

Let's continue with our bicycle faux pas reference:

"It's 2018, and I'm riding my bicycle through Central Park. It's one of the first days of spring. The leaves are peeking out of the branches. There's a snap in the air and the aroma of new beginnings lilts softly on my nostrils. I push the pedals, getting my bike up to speed and a smile takes over my face. This. Bike. Loop. Is. Mine."

Quick Tip – Have fun with this. The details are the fun parts of the story. It takes some time to make sure you're sharing the important ones. For the record, you don't have to describe every single thing. Providing nuanced details specific to your story make it real. This is the magic that enables your audience to see themselves in the exact moment you're sharing.

And finally, the letter R.

R

The letter R in P.E.A.R. Method stands for Response.

Always elicit a response from your audience when speaking or telling stories. Get the audience involved! Tell stories that put the audience in the middle of the action. When you do, you'll build trust, demonstrate authority and have your audience wanting more. One of the best ways to introduce this is asking the audience to participate.

Let them see themselves as the hero in the story. Allow them to experience your emotions and challenges. Paint the picture of how things can change for them, like they did for you.

Here's an example:

"It's 2018, and I'm riding my bicycle through Central Park. It's one of the first days of spring. The leaves are peeking out of the branches. There's a snap in the air and the aroma of new beginnings lilts softly on my nostrils. I push the pedals, getting my bike up to speed and a smile takes over my face. This. Bike. Loop. Is. Mine."

You can elicit a response by asking the audience questions like: "Show of hands, how many of you can relate?" or "Do you remember that last time you had a great day at the park?"

Objection Handling by Covering the A.R.E.A With P.E.A.R.

So let's tie it all together: we'll combine The A.R.E.A Framework and the P.E.A.R. Method to handle the three classic sales objections. Please note that we'll install the P.E.A.R. Method into the Evidence portion of the A.R.E.A. Framework.

"It's Too Expensive"

We'd use a client Milestone story:

> A: I understand your concerns here. The price is actually a great value.
>
> R: The reason is, one of our best clients had the same concern before she signed up with us.
>
> E: Sarah runs a midsize agency serving clients globally just like you do. I remember speaking with her like it was yesterday. When I hop on the call, Sarah's stress is clear. Her brow furrowed, shoulder's tight and I can tell that she's distracted.

I greet her and ask how she's doing. From her first response it's obvious that her business is running her and not the other way around.

We dive into her current stresses and what they're doing to her and to her business. It becomes plain that our program is exactly what Sarah needs to get out of her own way. When it comes time to talk about the investment of the program, Sarah balks, saying it's too expensive for her.

I walk her through two of our frameworks that will help her with exactly where she is. And we discuss what could happen if she doesn't change. Sarah agrees to commit the results future Sarah wants. Using our Frameworks, Sarah got her investment back in six weeks and she's on her way to getting a 5x ROI in just 90 days.

> A: And that's why our price is well valued for someone in your position.

Does that sound like something you like to see happen in your business?

"Is This Going To Work For Me?"

Mission stories work well here:

> A: Based on what I've heard from you so far, a service like this would work really well for you.

> R: That's because that's exactly why we built this company. The goal is to make it easy for consultants to grow their business while focusing on what they do best – consulting.

> E: I remember starting my career as a consultant a decade ago. I'm green, I have no idea how to bring in clients. I'm unclear about my offer. I'm treading water and I can tell that there has to be a better way. In the rare instance that I do get a prospect on the phone, I'm stressed out about what will happen if they say yes.

I remember getting lucky and signing my first client. I'm standing there excited and the excitement quickly turns to dread. I have to do this over and over again and I don't know what to do. I decide then and there that I need to have a repeatable system to streamline my operation. Lo and behold, ten years later, we're growing with 50+ happy clients. And I get to help consultants like you hit their first seven-figures, all while working less.

> A: If you want to get back to working on the business and not in the business, this program will work wonders for you too.

Does that resonate with you?

"I Don't Know If Now Is The Right Time"

Vision stories work well for this objection:

> A: It's actually a great time to get started.

> R: The reason is, we've engineered this system specifically to accelerate quick wins. Each of our new clients receives a step-by-step action plan and the sooner the plan is set up, the faster we can get you to your goals.

> E: Let me take you back five years ago. I'm sitting in my home office and see a text message from Gary – a new client.

His message says:

> *"Dude, I'm barely three weeks in to the program and it's already night and day in my business. I have clarity, I have systems and I know what to do next. I can't believe I didn't think it was the right time. Excited for what comes next. Thank you."*

I start digging into our client portfolio and start analyzing the time to results. On average, new clients see results within three weeks of getting started. They find that it frees up much more time in their business.

Clients who wait, often stay confused spending more time and resources.

We're building a community of seven-figure consultants who focus on what they do best.

> *A: That's why it's actually a great time to get started.*

Can you see that happening for your business?

Use *The Superpower Storytelling Workbook* A.R.E.A. Framework exercises to build these skills and make them habits.

Get it here:

Scan the QR Code with your phone!

You've learned how to turn your ideas into crisp statements that move people to swift and decisive action. Well done!

Now it's time to get your customers excited to buy.

CHAPTER 5

Getting Your Customers Excited To Buy

Your customers are excited to buy when:
You demonstrate an understanding of their pain
points and their desired outcomes, so that you're
able to verbalize them in the form of an offer they
can't resist.

Ever woken up in the middle of the night to find that you fell asleep on the couch in the living room with the TV still on?

Picture yourself waking up groggily. Turning your head and having a look at the dancing light box to see an infomercial.

On the screen is a picture showing a transformation from a home fitness program. You rise up on your elbow to bring your eyes back in focus. The screen flashes a few more newly-chiseled bodies. The voiceover touting the benefits, the ease and the opportunity.

Somehow you can't look away. You place your hands around your own mid-section as you survey the toll free number on screen. You're fully awake now.

You're watching an infomercial for something called P9ox. P9ox is an at-home fitness workout system designed to get epic results in just 90 days.

For those unfamiliar with P9ox, that means one of three things:

- You get a great night's sleep most nights and haven't been up late enough to catch the classic infomercial,
- You've already got a robust workout routine, or...
- I'm aging myself and P9ox is before your time.

P9ox became one of the most popular at-home workout programs in history. Their storytelling magic was a shining example of successfully nailing what their customers think, feel and want. And it turned the Beach Body Company into a multi-billion dollar fitness brand on account of it.

How did they get there though? Let's run the infomercial through the *Superpower Storytelling Framework* to see:

- It all starts with labeling what's at stake for their audience. Even the most seasoned fitness enthusiasts notice they're not making progress with their workouts after a certain point. The infomercial shows the audience what will happen if they don't change: They'll be stuck on a plateau. P90x helps the audience understand: "Why do I plateau with traditional workout programs?" With the stage set, P90x primes the audience for question number 2.

- What does the audience want to learn or achieve?:

  - Watchers of the P90x commercial are hooked. The infomercial promises to help viewers answer: "How can I continue to get visible results from my workouts without plateauing?" With the audience's goal properly outlined, the marketers at P90x are able to set the stage for an emotional commitment from viewers.

- The marketers behind P90x create the emotional space by labeling how they want the audience to feel:

  - P90x labels the pain point of work out plateaus with a name so that the audience can feel understood and informed. P90x calls this plateau: muscle confusion. (I'm not sure this is a real term, but it's a great term for those watching the infomercial to say, "Yeah, that's what I'm experiencing. I have muscle confusion." (Naming a symptom or pain point helps the audience feel seen and understood creating a bridge between a viewer and a product, service or brand.)

  - The infomercial further explains why previous solutions don't work: Workouts don't change or adjust to give the body more results. The explanation deepens the understanding of "muscle confusion" and creates a gap for the audience between their current muscle confused state and the results they're seeing from workouts.

- With the framework firmly in play, the infomercial makes its most important move:

- The infomercial uses question 4: What do you want the audience to do next?

    - Throughout the infomercial you are shown testimonials of clients boasting incredible transformations once they've solved their "muscle confusion."

    - P90x leverages testimonials and explanations of their workout program to invite people to call now to experience their own transformation over the next 90 days.

    - The rest is history.

Beach Body tested 14 different versions of their P90x infomercial before finding the right one.[43] Talk about testing your message!

P90x helped their audience tell their own story better by a demonstration of what's at stake – the cost of inaction, dissecting the pain points, labeling them and offering a solution with a clear call to action.

And they made their case, offering a clear and differentiated solution to the problem deploying the *Superpower Storytelling Framework* flawlessly. P90x is a great example of a brand speaking directly to the story a prospect tells about their own life and driving them to take swift and decisive action.

Now let's talk about how you can clarify and make your own home run offer.

Clarifying Your Offer

Clarifying your offer starts with solving a simple equation:

$$(wp(f)w)\backslash wn = S$$

You're likely thinking, wait a second... This is a book about storytelling... I'm confused. How the heck did math get in here?

Don't worry.

This isn't a math equation.

It's an equation to help you dive deeply with your audience, build trust quickly and communicate your message clearly.

- wp = What problem are you solving?
- (f)w = For whom?
- wn = Why now?
- S = Sales

Regardless of your role, at some point you'll want to push forward an initiative. That goes whether you're an employee, a consultant, an executive, a business owner or something else.

The big question that you must answer before all others is: What problem do you solve for your prospects? You must be aware of the problem for your audience, aka, whoever's buying in or saying yes to your proposal. What variable do they want to solve for? What is the problem they have right now?

How can we articulate that problem in a manner that gets them prepared to take action on it? That's the place we need to start from.

This is how we'll approach your marketing. How we'll build sales scripts. How we'll tailor your message to create a reason for your prospects to interact with your brand. It's our job to discuss what's important to our prospects. To show understanding for the issues, problems and mindset they currently experience.

The sooner we can prove ourselves trustworthy, the sooner we can start solving their problems.

To further demonstrate the effectiveness of the "equation," let's jump into Taki Moore's Problem Stack.

The Problem Stack [43]

The Problem Stack is a framework designed to help you access the three levels of a problem as your audience/prospect experiences it – giving you a clear method to agitate the pain, demonstrate understanding and offer a corresponding solution.

Let's start with level 1.

The Known Said Problem

The Known Said Problem is the common knowledge problem that your audience experiences. Everybody knows that the problem in question is an issue.

For example, let's say our audience is fast-growing startups. It's common knowledge that prioritization in fast-growing startups is a difficult proposition. Everyone knows this. That's not new information, but it is something your prospects may relate to. Think of this as level one in your messaging. We're talking about the problem they know they have. Mentioning problems at this level doesn't cause ground-breaking realizations for your audience.

This is the contextual level on which you must base your storytelling. Startups are hard, but what specific aspects of startup life are hard?

When we dive down to level two, that's when our prospects will start paying attention. That's when we get down to The Known Unsaid Problem.

The Known Unsaid Problem

This is the problem your prospects know that they have but would never speak about in public. Unless there's real trust. This is the problem they're afraid of. This keeps them awake at night.

There might even be some shame associated with this problem in their mind. The prospect doesn't know what to do next.

In keeping with our fast growing startups example, a level 2, Known Unsaid Problem might be: That startups in a particular sector are experiencing a great deal of employee churn. The company is losing great talent to the competition and, as a result, their growth projections are in peril.

Demonstrating this secondary level of problem awareness creates an "I'm not alone" situation. You can gain the trust of your prospect, meet them where they are and form an emotional connection with, you guessed it; storytelling.

And then finally we have The Unknown Unsaid Problem.

The Unknown Unsaid Problem

Unknown Unsaid Problems are the deepest level of messaging.

Understanding Unknown Unsaid Problems differentiates you in the marketplace. Once you show your unique angle of understanding to your prospects, they can't unsee it. It's a true demonstration of what's at stake. It becomes the filter through which they see everything else in their business.

In our fast-growing start up example, the Unknown Unsaid Problem might be that the root cause of employee churn is usually predicated on two distinct criteria, 1) lack of training for employees (training makes employees feel seen, heard and that their skills can contribute to the mission of the company), and 2) poor management with no cohesive culture (lack of management sets the tone for employees to make a swift exit).

How about in your industry?

Open up your workbook and let's work through the Problem Stack together.

This exercise will help you clarify:

- What you have to offer
- Who your audience is

And by the end of this exercise, you'll know:

- What problem you're actually solving
- How to create a new lens from which your prospects can view their problem, and...
- Why you are the best person to solve that problem for your prospects

This exercise will help you prepare for any blockers or surprises.

Take a few minutes to outline these three problems. You'll need these later.

Once you've worked through the Problem Stack, let's take a moment and dive into seven magnificent reasons our prospects open up their wallets.

The Magnificent Seven Reasons Why People Buy

Whether you're selling business to businesses (B2B), business to consumer (B2C) or direct to consumer (D2C), you're selling to a person at the end of the day.

Never forget that there's another human being on the other side of a sales interaction. That human being is looking to solve a problem or pain point. Keeping this top of mind will give you an advantage in the market.

There are seven core reasons why people buy anything. Businesses buy goods and services for four reasons. Consumers buy goods and services for three reasons. If we use storytelling to outline these seven reasons, we're able to articulate why our prospects should care. That's the all-important first step to becoming the go-to person for the problem that you solve.

The Four Reasons Why Businesses Buy: B2B

1. Make More Money

A business invests in a product or service if it will make them more money. Plain and simple. Does your solution help your prospect make more money? If so, how and how much more money can they expect to make by investing in your solution?

Let's have a look at HubSpot as an example. HubSpot is a marketing / CRM software. HubSpot helps businesses collect, organize and market to their contacts.

HUBSPOT:

To make the world Inbound. We want to transform how organizations attract, engage and delight their customers.

If you look at their tagline, we can see that HubSpot is here to help their clients make more money.

> "To make the world inbound. We want to transform how organizations attract, engage and delight their customers."

It's clear that HubSpot helps businesses to attract more money by helping them to engage and delight.

The tagline is an easy value proposition to follow all the way to the bank.

From here we know what types of stories to tell.

2. Save Money

The second reason a business invests in a product or service is to save money. Are your prospects currently using a process that costs them a ton of money? Are they using too many people inside of the organization to handle a specific function? Is there a way to do it more cost effectively?

Can your solution cut the amount of hours your prospects need to spend in half? Can your solution help them to save on hiring costs?

Here's an example from InVision App, a design software that gives companies the ability to mock up digital assets without writing code.

INVISION:
We help companies of all sizes unlock the power of design-driven product development. InVision gives teams the freedom to design, review and user-test products — all without a single line of code.

"We help companies of all sizes unlock the power of design-driven product development. InVision gives teams

the freedom to design, review and user-test products – all without a single line of code."

If you've ever worked with developers you know that their skillset commands a high price. The phrase "all without a single line of code" demonstrates how InVision saves companies money. They no longer need developers to test their designs.

If InVision can help their customers make progress without developers, it's clear they help their customers save money.

Great stories to tell about this are how much money or time a prospect can save by using this product or service.

The idea is to help your prospects understand – through stories – that they too can achieve similar results.

3. Increase Efficiency

The third reason a business invests in a product or service is to increase efficiency.

Are results high input but low output? Is a current process causing lots of hiccups and headaches? (For example, mailing blueprints across the country overnight instead of sending them electronically.) Think of everything that could go wrong in shipping – damage, delays, sending the wrong files, etc.

Inefficiency is bad for business, not to mention that it's expensive. Efficiency creates simplicity by removing variables from processes.

Our example from DataDog, a cloud monitoring service, illustrates that point:

DATADOG:

The DataDog team is on a mission to bring
sanity to IT Management.

"The DataDog team is on a mission to bring sanity to IT management."

Sanity is a euphemism for order and efficiency. When things are insane, they're chaotic and out of order. By using DataDog, prospects gain clarity for their IT management. Clarity means better results and less time, energy and resources wasted on opaque systems and processes. This means more money for the company.

Does your product or service provide efficiency and clarity to your customers? Then Milestone and Mission stories will help you to articulate how your products or services deliver on that promise. These stories will show that you understand their pain and get your customers excited to buy.

4. Mitigate Risk

The fourth reason a business invests in a product or service is to mitigate risk. Risk mitigation is one of the most overlooked value propositions in business, but that doesn't undermine its importance. It's so important, in fact, that there are full-on risk management departments at many companies. The department's sole function is to analyze the company's exposure to downside risk.

Can you help your prospects assess risks they're unaware of? Can you lower their exposure in the event of downside? Are you able to help them capitalize on opportunities when the rest of the market soaks in the downside?

If so, you have a solution of massive value to your prospects.

Our example, Caterpillar, the world's largest manufacturer of construction equipment, illustrates this to a T:

CATERPILLAR:
Our mission is to enable economic growth
through infrastructure and energy
development, and to provide solutions that
support communities and protect the planet.

As their tagline suggests, "Our mission is to enable economic growth through infrastructure and energy development, and to provide solutions that support communities and protect the planet." The word "protect" implies low risk. Lower risk means that systems or processes are codified and are going to work with minimal issues.

Those are the four reasons that businesses buy anything. Each of these reasons is measurable. When you can couple metrics with storytelling, you're sure to make your solution stand out. If you're able to get your prospects to share specific data around these four B2B reasons, you can make the stories real to their situation and you can always cite what they told you.

This allows you to speak directly to their specific business case. It demonstrates respect and builds rapport.

Another scenario to consider is decision-making inside of a company. Research shows that buying decisions include 6.8 people inside of an organization. Meaning each stakeholder in a buying decision may hold importance for a different metric and value proposition depending on their role.

You need to be able to cite how what you do ties back to the specific wants and needs of their individual role.

This is where storytelling comes in. This helps you resonate and look like an expert. You'll be able to explain how your solution solves your prospect's specific problem.

When you're ready, let's take it a step further – let's bring in the Judo of consumer-based buying decisions.

The Three Reasons Why Consumers Buy: B2C

There is no shortage of solutions, options and trends in the B2C ecosystem. Even though competition is steep and margins are slim, there are three key reasons why consumers buy. More than likely, you yourself have bought something based on at least one of the reasons listed below. You are human after all.

Let's jump into consumer buying behavior.

1. Better Health

One reason consumers buy is to achieve better health. Consumers love products that will help them live a healthier life. Unfortunately, this sheds little light on whether they will use the product or service. That's a whole other issue beyond the scope of this book.

The idea is that the products or services you sell will help to form or change the habits that lead to living a healthy lifestyle. Think exercise, eating well, looking good, etc. These are classic motivators for consumer purchasing.

Let's take a look at an example from a company that promotes better Health. If you remember, earlier in our *Superpower Storytelling Journey* we shared a story about small company out of Portland, Oregon, called Nike.

Nike uses the tagline:

> *"To bring inspiration and innovation to every athlete**
> *in the world.*
>
> **If you have a body, you are an athlete."*

NIKE:

To bring inspiration and innovation to
every athlete* in the world. *If you have a
body, you are an athlete.

This line speaks to the aspirations of many. Traditionally, "athletes" wake up early, adhere to strict diets and practice their craft two-to-three times a day for decades. The results?

Pristine physical condition and multimillion dollar contracts. Yet, that's not most of us.

In one way or another each of us aspires to be – in our own way – like one of the many successful athletes that endorse their products. That's what Nike is selling.

It's what the brand says about our aspirations for better health that brings people into the fold. Nike helps us tell ourselves that we, too, are athletes because we, too, have bodies.

Now let's explore the second reason consumers buy.

2. More Wealth

The second reason consumers buy is to create more wealth.

Products or services that help people to level up on their finances – or make it easier to do so – are always in style. Think about it, would you like to make more money? Would you like to have more money for yourself or your family?

More money to invest in your kids, or to start that real estate portfolio you've always dreamed about? Or would you like to have enough money to buy that RV and take a cross-country road trip?

Did you recently leave a job because you got a better offer?

Whatever that thing is, the idea of making more wealth will lead each of us to make potential purchasing decisions. Wealth is something people will always want more of. Wealth signifies control, power, access and freedom. These are some of the important status builders that consumers seek.

Let's take a look into Charles Schwab.

CHARLES SCHWAB:

Helping investors help themselves.

Charles Schwab has over 40 years of experience helping investors steward their finances. It says so in their tagline.

"Helping investors help themselves."

If you're investing with Charles Schwab, they're helping you to get more out of your financial investments. Which should translate to more wealth in the long run. When you invest, it's like buying yourself a day that you do not have to work in the future. With more wealth you can have less stress. Building more wealth takes sustained planning and discipline over many years.

Products or services that help to build wealth, lead customers toward building a better future. That's something most will pay a good price for.

3. Stronger Relationships

The third reason consumers buy is to build stronger relationships. Do you help people to build, maintain and grow fulfilling relationships? If so, you'll always sell well.

Why? What good is better health or having more wealth if there aren't great people to share it with?

Now let's talk about having stronger relationships.

You've heard of Instagram. I'm won't argue whether social media platforms may actually destroy relationships. That's a whole other can of worms again that are well beyond the scope of this book. It's an argument that will go on for many years to come. However, that's not the purpose of this exercise. There's plenty of resources that can speak from a more informed perspective about that subject (i.e., *The Social Dilemma* or *Why You Should Delete Your Social Media* by Jaron Lanier).

However, I digress. You may draw your own conclusions. Back to Instagram.

Look at the tagline:

INSTAGRAM:
Capture and Share the World's Moments.

Instagram's goal is to improve relationships by capturing and sharing the world's moments.

Everyone in the world experiences moments. Sharing those moments brings synergy between people. Synergy builds strong relationships and creates space for building trust.

These are the three reasons consumers buy anything.

Earlier, I mentioned a "judo" application for the seven reasons people buy...

We get into "judo" if you're selling B2B, leveraging the four B2B reasons and you can combine the B2B reasons with the Consumer buying reasons for your individual prospect.

Here's what I mean.

Let's say your business helps your customers to make more money. How does making more money for the business help the individual to whom you're selling? Will it help her to have more personal wealth, have better relationships because she's no longer working 16 hours a day?

Selling to solve the problems in the business AND to the person's specific need makes you stand out. Scratch below the surface to learn more about the person behind the problem. This is where storytelling and building rapport can take a deal deeper.

Asking open-ended questions will get you there.

Here are a few to add to you quiver:

- Tell me more about that...
- Can you give me an example?
- How do you feel about that?
- How long has that been a problem?
- How much do you think that's costing you?
- How does this affect you personally?
- What does that mean for you?

Questions of this nature allow your prospects to open up – naturally. They're not limited in their responses.

Open-ended questions show that you're listening. Further, they can give you A LOT of data about a prospect. In turn, creating space for the emotions behind their business and unique problems.

For example:

Did your prospect just have a baby? That likely means they'll want to spend more time at home with their new addition.

Whenever I learn that a colleague or a prospect recently had a baby, I send them one of my favorite essays: Paul Graham's *Life Is Short*.[44]

The essay outlines the speed at which the magical moments of childhood pass for parents – calling parents to action to remember that life is indeed short. The article is a cogent reminder to stay home with your family and enjoy every last second.

What does this mean for the business?

We're going to share how our solution helps the company to make more money. And how implementing the solution will increase the efficiency of the entire department. Increased efficiency for the department means fewer late nights at the office. The prospect can spend more time at home.

Spending more time at home will increase the quality of their relationship with their family. The prospect won't stress about staying home with their new child. You helped the business and your solution also took care of the prospect's personal problem.

It takes a series of probing questions to access this level of problem understanding. When you get there, you become a trusted partner.

Knowing what story threads to pull out from your prospects and which stories of your own to share. Knowing which stories will get them locked in on who you are, not solely on what you have to offer their business. That way you'll be more than a vendor, more than a colleague. It starts with listening.

These are the magnificent seven reasons that people buy anything. You should use each of them. Use the workbook to make tag-lines for your value prop as it applies to each one.

If you do this correctly, you can bring the three consumer buying reasons into a B2B sale.

How, you ask? Well, who do we sell to, or try to convince to follow along with our initiatives? Other Humans, that's who! When we approach a sale this way, that makes us a good partner and it makes your solution a good investment.

You know exactly how to talk to anyone in any company – of any size – about the why behind what you have to offer. Now you can show how it can affect their bottom line and their story.

Most importantly, though, it means we're playing long-term games with long-term people. That's how you build customers for life. That's how you get your customers excited to buy.

Now let's jump in to some practical tips and applications for storytelling inside of your business.

Storytelling Exercise

Open up your *Superpower Storytelling Workbook* to The Magnificent 7 Reasons Why People Buy.

Take a moment and jot down in your workbook some of the ways your solution makes your prospect more money, saves them money, increases efficiency or decreases their risk.

Then take a shot at outlining how helping their business to achieve better results can impact the human on the consumer side.

Are your methods or results quantifiable? If so, this will make it easy for your prospects to understand why it's in their interest to invest.

Get your workbook here:

Scan the QR Code with your phone!

CHAPTER 6

Practical Storytelling Tips And Real Life Applications

Forming the habits of great storytelling and applying them to your business

In his best-selling book *Outliers,* Malcom Gladwell breaks down the research of Swedish psychologist Anders Ericsson who claims that mastery – of a skill – takes 10,000 hours.[45]

You can break that down into any combination of years and hours per week:

- 5 years of 40 hours a week
- 10 years of 20 hours a week
- 15 years of 15 hours a week
- 20 years of 10 hours a week
- or any other combination of consistent time

However, there are two important factors that Gladwell's rule of 10,000 doesn't state:

- Quality of practice can significantly diminish the time to mastery. Perfect practice makes perfect.

- Practice is a mentality. I contend that actively thinking through the development of a skill, even if not practicing directly, can count toward those 10,000 hours.

For example:

On average, women speak 16,215 words per day and men speak 15,669 words per day.[46] That's about five hours of talking... per day. Let that sink in. That adds up to over 35 hours of speaking per week. Depending on your age and vocation, you're already a master at speaking if you think about it.

You've got great content, so now it's time to command authority and make people pay attention. We'll leverage everyday life situations to practice our storytelling skills.

Let me show you a few examples:

Getting Yourself Warmed Up

Okay, we should talk about warming up. Warming up before we talk is essential to powerful communication.

Do you remember when your voice would crack in high school while presenting at the front of the class? I can't forget. I think about it like starting an engine cold, sprinting before you've stretched and gotten your heart rate up or addressing a group of people before you've had your coffee... Could you pull it off? Yes, but would you get optimal performance? Likely not.

This is why we warm up. I'll share a few quick exercises to warm up the voice and the body.

I perform these exercises before events, workshops, presentations or podcasts. They work whether you're on stage or in virtual meetings. Personal voice and body exercises and twisters to practice your diction.

Diction is how you say certain words. Diction demonstrates clarity in your speech and shows confidence. I'm dating myself here, but as children we would spar with tongue twisters on the playground.

Remember:

> *"How much wood could a woodchuck chuck if a woodchuck could chuck wood?"*

This is diction at work.

Have you seen the movie *Anchorman, The Legend of Ron Burgundy*, starring Will Ferrell? It's worth a watch and don't worry, I won't spoil it for you. There's a scene where Ron is sitting in front of the production team warming up.

He's making strange movements with his mouth and uttering "Unique New York" over and over. Ron is practicing diction. Unique and New York each have two syllables that tiptoe on top of each other.

They both require a strange movement in the mouth, not to mention they sound funny as well. They're a great mechanism to get you to be more successful and more measured in the way you deliver your words.

Here's a second example: "Red leather, yellow leather." An important note for practicing: it's not about going fast, it's about the clarity of your speech.

So it doesn't matter if you can stumble through the syllables. It matters if you can hear the syllables. Going slowly is actually the best way for you to practice this skill. Progress comes from saying the phrases over and over, speeding up more each time until you achieve mastery.

Speed

At what speed do you speak? I know myself, I speak quickly. That's authentic to me. Sometimes though, I speak too quickly. If you speak too quickly, you can gloss over the intention of the words for the people who you're speaking to.

To practice speed, practice by slowing things down. Work on being extra deliberate with the words you say.

Here's why:

There's a certain pace that draws people into your stories. You'll notice that the rate of speech that you speak is a great indicator of how much people pay attention. This will take some time for you to practice and get better at. So here are few ways to practice slowing down your sentences:

Method 1:

- Find a blog post, a piece of your content or one of your presentations.
- Pick a single line and read it aloud as fast as you can.
- Does it make any sense to you?
- Re-read the same line aloud. Now slow it down a hair.
- Repeat this process two or three times, slowing it down further and further each time.

Take note which one of those attempts feels the way that you want people to feel when they hear your stories. That's the one you should use. That's your pace. That's how you should speak for every story.

Method 2:

- Find a couple of pens or pennies.
- Place them in your opposite hand.

- Find a blog post, a piece of your content or one of your presentations.

- Pick a single line to read aloud.

- Remove a pen or penny from one hand and place it on the desk while saying a single word from your chosen line.

- Do this as slowly as possible.

It will feel painfully slow to start but this is how we even out our pacing to create drama and engagement.

Cork Method

In ancient Greece, if you wanted the audience to hear you, you had to enunciate. To enunciate, you have to open your vocal system to project your message. Otherwise, the syllables of speech would be lost into the vast expanses of auditoriums or agoras.

The great orators of the day used the cork method to help with this. Here's how it works: take any cork from a bottle of wine. Place the cork between your teeth, and start talking. I usually pick up a book and read aloud. This gives you the capacity to improve multiple skill sets at the same time:

- Running words and phrases at different speeds.

- Reading aloud without sounding like you're reading.

- Body control. You'll notice quickly how tense your body becomes when you're speaking.

- How you say and express your words. When the cork is in your mouth, it will force you to think about how you say your words. You won't be able to use the normal techniques you use to speak and...

- Reading comprehension. You'll also take in new information and increase your intellect because readers are leaders.

Practice speaking with a cork in your mouth for five minutes a day to see your communication improve exponentially.

You'll also notice that there's a whole lot more depth and mileage in each syllable that you speak. Now that you're nice and warmed up, you're ready to communicate. If you're presenting or leading a workshop, I recommend warming up your audience as well.

Warming Up the Audience

Before workshops or training, I like to play a quick game. I've found that games – even virtually – are one of the best ways to get everyone on the same page.

The other important part of warming up is that it gives you control of the room. You have the trust of the people. Now they're yours to guide. Here are three of my favorite warm-up games to use in workshops:

Walk, Stop, Name, Clap

This is one of my favorite games to play as a warm up because everyone is seen acting silly. It puts everyone on the same page and opens the conversation up to sharing. The warm up works as well remotely as it does in person.

Purpose

Have hilarious fun with each other while following increasingly complicated instructions, guaranteeing fun and some of your participants getting it wrong.

Steps

- **Round 1:** Instruct people to walk around when you say "Walk!'" and stop walking when you say "Stop!" (do this for a minute or so).
  - If using this warm up in a virtual setting make the walking motion with your fingers
- **Round 2:** Instruct people to walk around when you say "Stop!" and continue walking when you say "Walk!"
- **Round 3:** Instruct people to – in addition to the rules from Round 1 – say their names when you say "Name!" and clap their hands when you say "Clap!"
- **Round 4:** Instruct people to – in addition to the rules from Round 2 – clap their hands when you say "Name!" and say their name when you say "Clap!" (Do

for a minute and have a laugh :). Now that everyone is on the same page their ready to learn.

You Are the Bus Driver

Purpose

This is a listening exercise. The key here is to see who in the audience is actually paying attention to the instructions. The whole trick to the game is in the title. No matter what information you share, the attendees themselves will always be the bus drivers.

Steps

Below you'll find a quick example. Feel free to update this information according to your own preferences.

- You are the bus driver.
- At your first stop, you pick up 29 people.
- On your second stop, 18 of those 29 people get off, and at the same time 10 new passengers arrive.
- At your next stop, 3 of those 10 passengers get off, and 13 new passengers come on.
- On your fourth stop, 4 of the remaining 10 passengers get off, 6 of those new 13 passengers get off as well, then 17 new passengers get on.
- What is the color of the bus driver's eyes?

If you're paying attention, the answer should be clear... it's right there in the title... You are the bus driver.

Moving Hands

This game works best in virtual settings. It's an easy opening gambit to bring the whole virtual room together. Full credit to Palladio Trusted Advisors AG.[47]

Purpose

To get the attendees moving, on the same page and in the process of working together.

Steps

Turn on Gallery view so that you can see all the attendees (Functionality works in Zoom, Google Meet, Microsoft Teams, etc.) Position your camera so that your face is centered, and you've got space on every side. Place your hand somewhere near your head: Above, below, to the left, right or anywhere in between. (Make sure to demonstrate how to do this for the attendees.)

Instruct the attendees to pick another person whose image they see on the screen as their reference. Attendees can choose any hand position to start once you give the word.

Once the action starts, the goal is to position your hand opposite to where your reference person holds their hand.

Example: If your reference holds their hand to the left, yours should be on the right; if above, position yours below. If your reference decides to move, you move too but make sure to keep it opposite of their position 100% of the time. (Demonstrate)

Check in with everyone so they know where they have to move their hand. After 45 seconds to one minute, stop the game, debrief, then jump into your workshop.

Planning a Presentation

There's no place where storytelling is more relevant, important and a value add than in the most public-facing document of your company – your deck. Your deck is how you get the attention of customers, how you create fear of missing out with investors and how you rally your team to excellence.

That's why we should plan presentations with story in mind. We'll discuss two different types of presentations here, our sales presentation and workshops/ trainings.

Get a free copy of my *Presentation Planning Cheat Sheet* and example slide deck here:

Scan the QR Code with your phone!

Planning a presentation requires a series of components that, when combined, form a complex web – a web that gets your audience excited and involved. Your attendees will become the star of the training/presentation.

You want people to get something out of your trainings and you want them to do the work to get it. We have a set outcomes for our audience. We're gonna work through all the categories that will help you deliver that outcome. The first thing to do is to label the frustrations of your audience by sharing a story that connects with the overall purpose or goal of the presentation.

Why are people here? Articulate those elements so people know exactly what they will accomplish by attending.

I recommend starting with some form of a warm-up game (see Warm Up Section). Host an activity to get people working together before the presentation/training starts. This is like an icebreaker. If virtual, you can ask a question and have your attendees jump into the chat. If you're live and in person, you can have them get up and walk around the room.

I've found that getting your audience into their body helps to control the session. It's a great way to get your group's attention and engagement early instead of hoping they'll listen. If you're delivering a sales presentation you can leave this section off.

Let's move on to Objectives:

Objectives

The next section is objectives. I like to lay out all of the training objectives. This is usually done in the form of a slide that says something to the effect that:

During the session we'll cover ....

- Main Point 1
- Main Point 2
- Main Point 3

"During the session we're gonna cover..." Then outline the presentation via bullet points for each section. This is important because it sets the tone for why your audience is here. And it frames everything in a nice and succinct package.

People are busy and busy people like order and structure. Setting expectations about time investment, shows respect for our audience's time. An objectives slide allows people to know what you're doing and why.

If running a workshop, after the objectives slide, create a slide asking for audience engagement. I ask: Which topic resonates the most? Once the audience tells you what resonates the most with them, you'll know which sections to spend more time on as well as where to provide clarity and where to ask for more engagement.

Then it's time to set expectations.

Expectations

If you're running a sales presentation, you can also leave this section out. Expectations for your training can be whatever you like. Though for my own workshops, I have five slides.

These slides allow you to say what you expect out of your audience during the session.

This sets the tone. For example my slides read:

Slide 1: "Share Your Ideas"

Invite conversation. Explain why sharing ideas is important. We can only learn together if we are able to get people to share. So give your audience permission to share their ideas.

Slide 2: "Be Honest"

Invite your audience to be honest. Invite them to share exactly where they are without filters and without fear.

This helps engagement and helps people feel seen. When there's an expectation of honesty, if you've done it right, you're going to create a space of comfort.

Slide 3: "Ask Questions"

Invite the audience to raise their hands and to jump in and ask questions at any time.

Slide 4: "Expect Value"

Set the expectation that the audience will leave with something to implement immediately.

Something that will get results – fast.

Set the expectation that you know why they're spending valuable time with you.

Slide 5: "Expect fun"

Play a game at the beginning of the training to get your attendees warmed up and involved.

Best practices are to include at least two types of activities in a one-hour workshop.

Activities break up the presentation. They're the key to allowing the attendees to do the work. This way we don't have to teach 100% of the time.

It keeps the energy up and gets the attendees to build the value they will take home with them after the training.

Learning new information is great, but having fun while you learn locks in the lesson. It also helps you to leave people with a positive association toward your message. Set expectations for your group and watch them fall into your message.

Introduction

Hi, I'm {Your Name}

- Business Stats
- Interests
- Resuls
- etc

Now it's time to introduce yourself. Let people know who you are and what qualifies you to be able to speak on the topic you're going to share. Pro Tip: Personal quips are fair game at this stage. You can share one of *"The Three Stories You Need to Lead"* right here.

If you're short on personal accolades and work for a company, you can always cite their credentials.

Transitions

Transitions are how we move from one topic to the next with ease.

Build a bridge between topics like expert DJs who move between songs, combining rhythm and key changes to keep the party flowing.

There's an art to this but here's the fastest way I've found. Restate a feature of the introduction story.

Smooth transitions show expertise.

Please avoid filler words like: umm, so, you know, etc. Filler words are among the most distracting and ugly things you can do when presenting. Nothing removes credibility and authority from your message faster. Imagine you were reading this very book and every five words you'd see "Umm."

> *"Then when I was explaining more, I'd UMMMMM, you know, move because the most important part is UMMM..."*

You'd place the book in the circular file (the trash) where it should go. Then you'd head to Amazon where you'd bestow a befitting one-star review.*

Debrief

Which on of these resonates the most?

The debrief or digest is an important part of workshops. It gives the group a chance to weigh in on what they just did. Then we'll play another game or do another activity; and whenever we play a game or do an activity, we do a post-game debrief. Ideally invite two or three people to share what they learned, felt or got out of the activity.

This accomplishes three objectives:

1. It's a way to facilitate conversations among the people who are participating in your presentation.

2. You'll learn the conversational language your audience uses to speak about their problems and their solutions.

3. Feedback is the breakfast of champions.

Head to Amazon and rate this book and leave a review. Five stars preferred but I'd appreciate any review;).

The debrief works well if you're building marketing material. Pay attention to every piece of feedback you get.

These can become your anecdotes for future presentations, marketing materials and your milestone stories. Our goal is to get people to share stories from their own lives and businesses to build a sense of community.

Summarize

You did it. You delivered a successful presentation. You shared plenty of valuable information. And the audience enjoyed it. It's time now to remind them what they learned. It's time to summarize the entire training.

There's an old expression about the three phases of a presentation:

- Tell them what you're going to tell them
- Tell them
- Then tell them what you told them

Summary is telling them what you told them.

We refresh their memory by going over each bullet that we've covered with a quick anecdote or quip for each.

Slide: "And now you know…"

> ### And now you know…
>
> - Main Point 1
> - Main Point 2
> - Main Point 3
>
> And that's how you're going to improve {INSERT TOPIC}

Great work.

Wait! There's one more thing. Now it's time for the most important part: your call to action.

Call To Action

Thank you

Ways to get in touch
- Your email address
- Your phone number
- Your website address

To make all your efforts worthwhile we need some way to measure success. We need some kind of conversion. We've got to make a clear call to action (CTA).

Your CTA will vary. It depends on your tribe, the topic of your presentation and the context in which you deliver it.

Here are a few example of CTA's:

- Book a session with our team.
- Head here to download our guide {lead magnet}.
- Sign up for our free training.
- Join our membership group.
- Buy my book.

For virtual presentations you can throw the link in the chat.

I always recommend adding a QR code to the final slide with a CTA. That way we can capitalize on the momentum, funneling folks toward action immediately.

The Sign Off

Before we leave the attendees, exit the stage or log out of the video conference, sign off with a quote and a thank you. This is a great place to drop your catchphrase.

I love this training framework because it gives the training lots of energy. Energy is the currency of an engaged audience. The best part? The structure does the heavy lifting for you.

I've received comments like: "Wow that was fun!" and "Your presentation is exactly the energy I needed!" and "Let's book you again."

I encourage you to try this format if you want to be clear, concise and prepared for your next presentation. For straight ahead sales presentations, you can leave out the activities. Unless it makes sense for your audience.

CHAPTER 7

How To Be The Most Interesting Person In The Room

The principles and practice of being the most interesting person in any room or on any podcast.

Dale Carnegie, in his classic *How to Win Friends and Influence People*, says simply: "To be interesting, be interested."

Re-read that sentence. There's not an ounce of fat on it. Is being the most interesting in the room really that simple?

Let's find out.

Take a moment and think about the most interesting person you've ever met...

What about them stands out to you?

I'm willing to bet that they exhibited some if not all of the following qualities:

- Made you feel important
- Asked great questions that got you thinking
- Listened more than they spoke, and listened with active curiosity and their full attention
- Knew how to read the room and bring energy to the conversation
- Told great stories and showed vulnerability
- Remembered and used your name

Interesting people are interested in others, in possibilities, in ideas and in stories. Interesting people have an intense curiosity about the world and everything in it.

Interest comes out in everything they do. Their interest flows in casual observations and in deep philosophical musings. That may or may not sound like you right now, but don't worry.

In this chapter, you'll learn how to be more interesting by leveraging who and what you are right now.

Delivery: How to Be the Most Interesting Person in the Room

The better you talk, the more money you make. The better you talk, the more opportunities you create for yourself. As a leader, the better you talk, the more endeared your team becomes to your shared mission.

The better you talk, the faster your company grows. The better you talk, the better your relationships are. It's worth noting that money is a great thing to have but money itself is not that interesting. Money is simply a result of providing value.

And money may not be the number one thing you're searching for and that's okay. If that's the case, feel free to substitute the word money with the result that YOU want.

But we'll continue explaining why the better you talk is so important. It's important to be able to speak well. To speak on and in the terms of those whose attention you seek. Storytelling is a bridge to help you get there.

I'll give you a quick quote: "If you want to speak to shepherds, you must speak of sheep." This is an example of how important it is to match the terms of your audiences with story. To lead your flock, you must have stories that provide context. Context creates clarity of mind and purpose. Clarity of mind and purpose creates clarity of action. Clarity of action leads to tangible results for you and your team, i.e., it will get you closer to what you want.

Open your workbook and jot down ideas around what you want to achieve.

These can be for your team, your business or with your family. Writing them down will help you get locked in on your leadership message.

Take a second and think about the most incredible orator you've ever heard speak. Think of someone you love to listen to. Someone who inspires you.

Some might say Steve Jobs or Brené Brown. Others may say Barack Obama, Oprah Winfrey, JFK or Dave Chappelle. For you, it could be your favorite Podcaster, YouTuber or TikTokker.

Have you got that person in your head? Okay. Now imagine that we stripped away the manner in which they speak and express themselves. Pretend you were reading the transcript of one of their speeches or performances.

Now let's reframe it with a few questions:

- Do you still believe this person?
- Do you trust this person?
- Does this person understand you?
- Does this person still inspire you?

Your answer is still likely yes.

Why? Because you're likely reading the transcript in the voice of your favorite orator. Their essence is present. They're able to outline exactly what's needed to help you get what you want from your life.

But if you were reading the text all by itself without the author's voice in your head or worse not knowing who the author was, you'd likely find the transcript marginal at best.

It is said that the spell of the tongue is the most dangerous spell of all.

That's why the ability to tell captivating stories is what separates market leaders from their competition. The ability to verbalize and speak those stories is an underutilized skill too few leverage.

As leaders, speaking is one of our primary tools for success. Declarative speech is important because it allows us to build trust. There's no better sales tool than the words you speak. And when combined, your words, intonation, and your body language ooze authority.

According to a study completed by psychologist Albert Mehrabian, only 7% of communication is conveyed through words. The remaining 93% is conveyed through nonverbal cues such as body language and tone of voice.[48]

Each of these elements adds up to your individual message. Their interplay is what makes you a leader. It's the creation of "the measured message" – tact, grace, style – but never without substance.

Does that sound like a skill you'd like to have? Then read on.

Here are a few techniques to help you sound like an expert, build trust with your audience and communicate your stories effectively.

First, let's remind ourselves who we're talking to:

- Who are these people?
- How do we show them respect, admiration and a mirror to see exactly where they are and where they want to be?
- How do we become the conduit to the better version of who they want to be?
- How do we show up with authenticity?

Next, we need to prime the pump. Here are a few examples that you can use and update to make your own. So make sure if you ever find a template or an example from someone else, don't copy it verbatim (I shouldn't have to say this in 2023, but I will.) What works for a tech startup founder, more than likely, won't apply to a seasoned corporate exec or to a holistic health coach.

Take the examples and apply them to your business – to your own context. You need only remember the principles and structure to leverage your newest superpower.

How to Make Others Feel Important[49]

Regardless of your title, station in life or your experience, the ability to make even those who come from different walks of life feel important will make you a memorable person and help you to win fans quickly.

One of the MOST underrated ways to make someone feel important is a good old fashioned compliment. Compliment something they accomplished, a fashion item they're wearing or a suggestion they made (please keep compliments appropriate). Compliments help others feel seen.

Another way is to ask someone to explain or teach you about their subject of expertise. Nothing makes someone feel more important than being publicly viewed as an expert.

Remind people how important they are to the Mission of whatever it is you're working on together. Making others feel a part of a bigger picture helps them feel important.

How to Ask Great Questions That Get Others Thinking

When you ask questions that get people thinking, they'll have no choice but to be authentic, because you're demonstrating an active curiosity about others and their lives.

Great questions separate the novice from the master. Great questions open people up and get them thinking. They have to answer genuinely. Open-ended questions and statements – phrases that don't have yes or no answers – work best.

- For example:
  - What are you excited about?
  - What's the highlight of your year so far?

- What character would you like to play in a movie?

I love questions like these for the following reasons. First, they're positive questions, meaning they take the recipient of the question to a positive place – thinking of and speaking of subjects they like and enjoy.

Second, it sets a barrier, in that if you ask questions like these and the person doesn't have any answers – exit stage left – they're low energy and not willing to be interested – even in their own lives. Conversations like these will be one-sided and energy intensive. There won't be much room for rapport here.

Third, when you get a person talking about themselves and things they like, they associate you, yes you, with those positive emotions. You're instantly more memorable because you took an interest.

How to Listen Actively

Active listening is the art of giving your undivided attention to a person or situation.

Remember the game *You Are The Bus Driver* we discussed in Chapter 6? We use the game to test if the audience is actively listening to the details provided.

A key metric in active listening is making someone not only be heard, but to feel heard as well. In these situations, a few examples would be to excuse yourself for a moment so that you can turn your phone on silent, to maintain eye contact with those you are in conversation with or if appropriate, take notes with pen and paper highlighting key points.

Before formulating a response to a subject or question, summarize what you hear.

Summarizing gives the clear indication you were listening and gives the person the feeling of authority to correct you if you missed an important point.[50]

How to Read the Room

I once had the misfortune of getting a keynote spot right after lunch at a conference in NYC.

I could see people in the crowd looking well fed, tired and losing steam. A full belly is a difficult energy to overcome. I knew I'd lose their attention if I didn't do something.

Thinking quickly I acknowledged the room and commented: "Hey, everyone! I know we've just had an incredible lunch catered by our sponsor, and I can see that it was so good that we're all digesting in comfort and we're a bit tired. That's okay, but I'll make a deal with you...

> "If you give me 100% of your attention, I'll give you 100% of my knowledge. Is that cool?"

The crowd agreed. Then I asked everyone to stand up for a second and stretch. The room laughed and that was it. They were locked into my presentation. The room needed a reset. I asked for their permission and the room obliged. Never be afraid to acknowledge the awkwardness of a situation if the room needs it.

Here are three key ways to read the room: Walk into a room with a hypothesis about what the energy/mood will be in the room. Actively observe the body language and expressions of others in the room.

Are people checking their phones? Are arms crossed and heads tilted to the side? Are the people leaning in toward you or are they leaning back? Closed off body language indicates a form of friction in your message. Work your hypothesis and leverage the agreement demonstrated above. Acknowledge the mood to disarm the friction if things are low energy or if there's low engagement.

How to Tell Great Stories, Show Vulnerability and Build Trust

Vulnerability is the currency of trust. Trust, like it or not, takes time to build. Consistently showing up as your authentic self when you speak to others is one of the key ways to build trust.

Many of the techniques we discussed in The P.E.A.R. Method (Chapter 4) are perfect to leverage in this case.

Authenticity can manifest itself by using descriptive language – the E, Emotions, and A, Atmosphere, from The P.E.A.R. Method – for example. And using them to share and take ownership over your mistakes.

Remember, the purpose of The P.E.A.R. Method is to take listeners along on a journey while you're experiencing it. Sharing your mistakes makes you relatable and makes your accomplishments more human.

If you're using active listening, you'll always build trust by knowing which stories to tell.

Remembered and Used Your Name

In the 1930s, advertisers created *"The Marketing Rule of 7"* which states that for a consumer to remember your product or service enough to buy it, they must hear it at least seven times.[51]

Times have changed significantly but seven is a good rule of thumb when applying it to names.

The sweetest sound a person can hear is his or her own name.

Showing a capacity to remember names is a differentiator. It shows that you care enough to remember.

According to Charan Ranganath, the director of the Memory and Plasticity Program at the University of California, Davis, the main reason we forget people's names is that we're simply not that interested in them.[52]

I know that sounds harsh, but it's true. We need to attach meaning to a fact, name or thought for us to do the cognitive work to create space in the mind for recall.

But don't worry, you're not the only one.

Here are three techniques I use to remember names.[53]

1. Word association:
   - Pair the name with an interesting fact.
   - Look at the person you're speaking to. Is the person wearing an interesting article of clothing or an accessory? Do they wear their hair in a specific way? Are they members of a specific profession? Where are they from?
   - Associate, i.e., Stephen Storytelling, or Stephen with the hair, Erin with big earrings, etc.
   - Repeat the word association with the name you just heard, five-to-seven times in your mind.

2. What part of the room did you meet the person? By the bar, at the buffet, next to the potted plant, etc.? Take a picture of the space in your mind and add the person to it. That way when you're racking your brain to remember a name you'll think of a space first.
   - Remember their name using the physical space you met them. The human mind has a greater memory for spaces than it does for names.

3. Can you spell it?
   - Ask the person to spell their name, and repeat the spelling back to them.

By leveraging these techniques you're tricking your brain into adding significance to the names your run into. The human brain works hard to forget information and filter out what's not absolutely essential. By doing this you're giving your brain a reason to remember.

Now that we've covered the basics of how to become the most interesting person in the room, let's dive into a more advanced and nuanced way to captivate: humor.

CHAPTER 8

Some Thoughts on Humor

How to approach making your audience laugh –
even if you're not funny

The Difference Between Jokes and Humor

Humor is an incredible device to build deep relationships. If you can get someone laughing, you can get them on your team. It's a classic. As such, it's importance can't be understated. Humor is deserving of a stand-alone chapter, albeit a short one.

However, humor is not something to take lightly. In other words, laughter is no laughing matter. It's an art form.

It takes a lot to be funny and nail it with jokes for your audience. For starters, telling jokes is different from being funny.

A joke takes place in a singular, unified moment. It's immediate. One can write a joke and use it in many circumstances. Telling a funny joke though, doesn't make YOU funny. Just like being a storyteller, being funny is a life path.

It's choosing to look at the world from a certain lens. In this case, the lens of funny. It's finding humor in everyday situations and circumstances. It's looking at your industry, your own stories or circumstances and satirizing the absurdity of them.

It requires fine-tuning your EQ and reading the room. It demands that you own your square and lose the fear of complete silence if there's no laughter. No easy task.

WARNING* If you choose to take this path, it will never stop. Your mind will be keenly aware that even in the most mundane of situations, there must be a joke to make.

And you'll be there looking for it. This will lead to you making more jokes. Testing the waters to see if your observations resonate with others. Sometimes it will not go well.

In truth, that's half the fun because when it does go well, there's no feeling quite like it.

And like most things in life, the wins outweigh the losses if we stay consistent.

That said, I enjoy performing standup comedy a great deal and writing jokes is one of the most difficult endeavors. Some jokes can take ten years to write. I see how much work it is to have an idea, massage that idea, test it out, fail with it over and over again until one day, it works.

Writing jokes takes a lot of conscientious effort and sometimes it's just not fun. If humor is a device you want to use, make sure you're willing to take your lumps. Some folks simply won't understand your sense of humor.

Now that we've got the disclaimer out of the way, Do you still want to be funny? Okay.

The first question to ask yourself is: Is humor on brand for you?

Let's unpack this a bit.

Your audiences, whether internal team members, customers, etc., will generally expect you to be some version of what you've always been. Remember our story about the UFC legend Chael Sonnen?

It's not that you can't change. If people don't know you as funny, they're less likely to laugh at your jokes even if they are funny. If so, here are a few structures that you can leverage.

The first thing to do is to start a collection of humor inspiration. Pull together your favorite quotes, jokes from professional comedians, comic strips and memes.

Save them somewhere and dissect the structure and what makes them great. See if you can spot the elements mentioned below. These resources can serve as a template for how to get started with your own writing and subject matter. They'll help you identify your own sense of humor.

I can't promise that you're going to be the next {insert your favorite comedian} but here are a few ways to win laughs. Try these on your next podcast appearance, while you're keynoting a conference, or even in a team meeting.

How to Approach Using Humor in Your Content

Humor works well in threes. Set up, set up, punchline.

The human mind responds well to threes. Anything over three pulls the mind out of the frame and you're giving too much information and risk confusing your audience. We count: 1, 2, 3, many.

If you're brave enough to attempt being humorous in your presentations or storytelling, let's break down a few examples you can use.

1. Let's start with a commonly held industry belief, a current event or feel free to leverage a particular topic that resonates with who you are and what you want to share.

2. Once you've identified the topic, start writing down some of the opposite ways to think about the topic.

I recommend writing down your main word or topic then branching off of it with words through free association. Note the absurd and leverage misdirection or double entendre. This is how we'll start to form our punchline. Don't worry if it's not funny yet. This can take a while. Humor comes from noting the absurdity and flipping the "normal" way an audience thinks about a subject.

- For example hint – the A.R.E.A. framework is your friend here.

- What's YOUR angle on the subject?

3. Use the angle to create your set up. We've got a direction to follow for version one of a punchline, now how are we going to get there? There are many ways to set up a joke but I'll let you guess... *Hint it's in the title of this very book. Storytelling of course! Which one of your three stories lends itself well to a possible punch line?

- Hint – The A.R.E.A. Framework strikes again. Our good old friends Reason and Example will help you craft a strong set up for your joke.

- Use that! It's a great way to craft a set up that is unique and on brand.

- Here are three examples of methods to structure humor:
    - Make it real
    - Make it relatable
    - Analogy

4. Don't quit. This is where the rubber meets the road with jokes and being funny. Keep editing and rewriting until you've got something pithy that feels right. When does it feel right? Trust me you'll know. Timing is essential for humor. A well-placed pause or varying the cadence of your words can make all the difference. Humor is all about reading the room.

5. Bring it to the world. The most difficult part about humor is that even if you think you've worked for years and crafted the perfect joke, the only way to know if it's funny is to test it. Test the concept in front of friends, family, and the local barista. Note how people react to it. Take that feedback and plug it back into what you've built.

I'd like to preface one again, that the joke writing process WILL take significant effort. So be ready for that.

Let's go over a few examples of how you can get started:

Joke Writing Ideas

I recommend starting by redefining common words, phrases or terms. Write down a few words or phrases from your industry or from your life. This will give your 'joke' broad application to many audiences. Listeners will make their own association with the words, phrases or terms. They'll do this based on their own previous experiences.

This is great for 2 reasons:

- You get to leverage mis-direction without forcing it - which is a must have in great jokes.
- Further you won't need to become a joke-writing savant to make something funny.

You need only craft a small story to set up context for the term. The easiest place to start is the acronym. Find one that you like and start redefining the words with some of your own.

Here are some examples of "jokes" using the A.R.E.A. Framework to kick us off:

Example #1

For our first example we'll start off with an example of a founder at a SaaS (software as a service) company:

Angle: I'm the founder of a SaaS company and dating is difficult.

Reason: I'm nerdy and often alone coding away trying to build my company.

Evidence: It's always been this way for me. I've been coding since the age of 12 and that makes me awkward in social situations.

Angle: And that's what's why it's hard for me to get a date as SaaS founder

On it's face that's a tough story however, we can turn tough into self-deprecating. Another go to for establishing authenticity. Let's redefine the SaaS (software as a service) acronym:

I'm a computer nerd. I've built software since the age of 12. It's hard to get a date... I live a SaaS Founder lifestyle. To some it means software as a service, but in my experience SaaS means: Sometimes alone, always single.

Not bad, not great but it's a start.

Example #2

Let's use marketing agencies and their ROI claims as our next joke subject:

Angle: A lot of marketing agencies talk about ROI, return on investment – but most agencies are all the same

Reason: They want to show that they're better than other agencies

Evidence: Most agencies don't do anything differentiated. They bark their claims like a pack of dogs.

Angle: And that's why a lot of marketing agencies are all the same.

What else could we make that acronym ROI mean?

Let's give it a shot:

Most marketing agencies bark their claims of delivering ROI. ROI. ROI. 90% of marketing agencies do in fact deliver ROI – Really Old Information. They give you nothing. Nothing new, nothing relevant and nothing timely.

We're different. Here's how we keep our information real time to get you the most up to date information.

Again, not bad and we're on our way.

Example #3

Let's have some fun with Example 3 and talk about going on vacation:

Angle: My wife and I took a vacation to a resort in Cancun so that we could spend some quality time together.

Reason: We needed some time away from our city life and the constant grind of commuting.

Example: We wanted to be as far away from work and the city life as possible. We made a pact to not wear shoes or socks for as long as possible.

Angle: That's why we chose Cancun to spend some quality time together.

For this example, let's go with the famous acronym NSFW-colloquially known as Not Safe For Work.

This acronym is a warning for inappropriate content or subject matter. You're already thinking of what it means and how inappropriate it this joke might be. That's further proves the magic of the natural misdirection with well-known acronyms.

Let's give it a shot:

Our vacation to Cancun was strictly NSFW - No Socks, Flip-flops Worn. We stayed on the beach ALL day. And when we weren't on the beach, we were in the hotel room and we didn't wear socks there either.

I rate each of these jokes at a 6 out of 10. They're not side-splitting by any stretch. If I were planning to perform them I would tweak parts and pieces. However, I think you get the point.

Find an acronym that you like, wrap it in one of your stories and start playing around!

Please keep in mind that the process is subjective and that everyone has a different sense of humor. Just because Group A laughs, doesn't mean Group B will and vice versa. There are no guarantees with humor. You may fail at it. And to be honest, you most likely will fail at it. But the thing is, if it's something you want to leverage, you're going to have to risk it.

And at the end of the day, the rewards of getting a laugh are worth it.

What's better than making your audiences smile?

Want training on joke writing for entrepreneurs? Send an email to stephen@stephensteers.com with the subject line "JOKES" and I'll get you more information.

Now let's close out this adventure and show you what to do next.

CHAPTER 9

What's Next

What to do now that you've invested in building
your newest superpower

You've made it! You've arrived at the first milestone of
your quest. Congratulations!

You are the hero in your own story and you've done the
work to earn your newest Superpower: storytelling.

You crushed it!

Like the mysterious woman in the opening story of Chapter 1, I hope that I've helped you to see something that you
couldn't see when you started on your quest. And with

your newly acquired vision you can help your audience see things in themselves they've never seen before.

I've proudly served as your guide throughout this book and we've uncovered a lot in our work together.

Now you know why you need to use storytelling if you want to build a sustainable business. You know what storytelling is because you've nailed characters, plot points, settings and themes and the hero's journey.

You're an expert at the *Superpower Storytelling Framework* and have a clear understanding of the questions you need to ask to create context for your three core stories. We spent some time clarifying your offer and digging below the surface of story with the Problem Stack.

You learned how to leverage the *Magnificent Seven Reasons People Buy* to get your customers excited to buy your solution or to buy-in to your ideas. You are on your way to becoming the most interesting person in the room using the *A.R.E.A Framework* and the *P.E.A.R. Method* to keep your content crisp and refreshing. We even covered how to create and interactive and memorable presentation and how to use humor to build deeper rapport with your audience.

I'm confident that through our work together that you know how to tell the stories you need to lead, sell and inspire.

Thank you for letting me be a part of your story.

First question is how do you feel?

Is there clarity in the way that you move?

Is there a different type of bond between you and your employees?

Are you more authentic in your communication?

Are you clearer on your personal brand?

I hope so. You've done the work. You've taken a huge step toward building out your brand by leveraging your story to do so.

Storytelling is now one of your newest Superpowers!

Congratulations!

When I decided to write this book it was because I saw many of the founders and sales people I work with missing this crucial skill.

No matter how incredible your products or services, none of that matters if you can't make people care. People don't care about the features – the bells, whistles and colors that you and your team spent the last six months building into your product.

Your audience cares about themselves. They care about their own problems and their own desired outcomes.

Theodore Levitt, former professor of Harvard Business School, once said:

> *"People do not want to buy a drill, they want to buy a hole." If you sell groundbreaking software, chances are no one cares about how your tech works – at least not initial-*

ly. The first thing on their mind is getting the results or the outcome that your solution offers.

Yes, they'll care about features later on, but it's going to take more time than you think. They'll care after they know you can solve their problem. It's your job to be clear about why your audience should care.

Taking it back to Levitt's quote: The drill is the tool they must buy to achieve the outcome they want – a hole.

Let's take the example a few steps further.

You've returned from a stint in the desert where you were lost for three days. You haven't eaten or had anything to drink in that time. As you wander back into civilization you pass a sandwich shop, and stumble inside. You're famished. Your legs are heavy, your stomach growls and your throat is bone dry.

If, upon seeing you, I offer to buy you a sandwich and a bottle of water, are you going to ask whether the beef was grass-fed? Are you going to investigate the progeny of the cow? Will you grill me about the processing standards of the cattle facility?

You might care about those questions, but you're not gonna ask them if you're starving. You're gonna do the natural thing... solve your immediate problem. You're gonna chug down that bottle of water and get started on that sandwich before anything else.

Only after you've satiated your hunger and thirst would you start to ask deeper questions. Then and only then – if ever – would you start asking about that grass-fed beef, the progeny of the cow, the quality of the facility, etc.

Storytelling optimizes for that mindset by giving us the context we need to show results. We're selling an outcome – aka – telling a story. We need to speak to solving the initial pain by providing the desired outcome.

By now you may be asking yourself the following questions...

I have a new Superpower... what now?

How can I continue to hone my powers?

I'm glad you asked! Here are a few ways I can help:

How to Continue Your Journey

All *Superpower Storytelling* resources are available at stephensteers.com/superpowerstorytellingbook or via the QR codes shown throughout the book.

Scan the QR Code with your phone!

FREE Nine-Day Speaking Course

Speak Yourself Into Existence – designed to give you the exercises and warm ups you need to feel confident every time you speak.

Sales Asset Review

Send me a recording of you delivering your sales deck and I'll provide comments. I'll do this for free for the first (5) five people who send an
email to: stephen@stephensteers.com with the subject line: "REFINE"

YouTube

Subscribe to my YouTube channel and say hi. I post content there on a regular basis. youtube.com/@stephensteers935 If you want more help here are a few ways to keep your knowledge going:

The "Context Selling" Accelerator

The outcome of the 100-Day Context Selling Accelerator is simple – to help founders build the key selling systems, strategies, stories and context needed to scale and eventually hand off sales. We'll get the job done with a distinct project focus, a mix of a synchronous asset review and personal guidance and accountability through one-on-one coaching. Send a quick email with the subject line

"CONTEXT" to stephen@stephensteers.com and I'll get you the details!

One-On-One Executive Coaching

If you're leading a seven-to-eight-figure company and you want to fire yourself from sales or make storytelling your leadership superpower, send a quick email with the subject line:
"COACHING" to stephen@stephensteers.com to explore working together one-on-one.

Team Training

Are you the CEO or VP of sales at a seven-to-eight-figure company? Want to refine the way you sell and rally your team to your best sales year ever? Then The Context Selling Method call review program might be a great fit for you. Send a quick email with the subject line:
"TEAM" to stephen@stephensteers.com and we'll
go from there.

Lastly, remember, as long as you are writing and sharing your story, the world is your oyster. Now get out there and tell yours. The world needs it!

See you soon!

Stephen

Acknowledgments

- Scott Sambucci – "For showing me the blueprint and generously guiding me each step of the way. Thanks for being you." Learn more about Scott's work at – salesqualia.com

- Dan Morris – "For mentorship, sharing knowledge and being a constant motivator." Learn more about Dan and his work at – mindracerconsulting.com

- The crew at Digital Undivided – Digitalundivided.com

- BELCHAM – Belcham.org

- Frank Hopper and Brett Luing at Capital Innovators – capitalinnovators.com

- Everyone in the Dynamite Circle, my favorite business community – dynamitecircle.com

- Marie Frochen – Ramp Up Lab – rampuplab.com

- Dov Gordan and JVMM – profitablerelationships.com

- Dov Baron – "For reminding me that there's nothing more important than being real."

- Andrea and Klaudia – "For friendship and amazing photographs"

- Rachel Resnik – "For encouraging me to lead with story." Learn more about Rachel's work at rachelresnick.com

- Trevor Greene, John Nader Adam Palmeter, Mariana Ramirez and Martín Leon – "For helping me find the laughter."

- Esther Jacobs – "For constant encouragement and for showing me your game-changing Reverse Writing technique." Check out Esther's work at reversewriting.com

- Larry Butler – "For patient and diligent editing on this manuscript."

- Uncle Willie, Alex Frantz Ghassan, Michael McKay, Oscar Cantu, Levy Reyes, Raul Wikkleing, Huggy and Drew, Priti Trivedi, Talog Morris- Davies, Valerie and Laurence VanDen Keybus, Evan Biller, Chris Henrichs, Dana Lindhal, Mads Singer, Jason Long, Victor Iraheta, J.P. Adechi, Mina Salib, Eric Daniel Horn, Vishal Agarwala, Fahad Al-Rashed, Olivier Rousseau, Mike Pierce, Christopher Fitkin and so many more!

Sources

Chapter 1

1   Medium. (2018). Malcolm Gladwell's Spaghetti Sauce Theory Applied to Presidential Candidates. Retrieved from https://medium.com/40fathoms/malcolm-gladwells-spaghetti-sauce-theory-applied-to-presidential-candidates-55479155807b

2   Wealthy Gorilla. (2022). Chael Sonnen Net Worth. Retrieved from https://wealthygorilla.com/chael-sonnen-net-worth/

3   Wikipedia. (2023). Chael Sonnen. Retrieved from https://en.wikipedia.org/wiki/Chael_Sonnen

4   The Schulz. (2021). Chael Sonnen: The American Gangster. [Audio Podcast]. Retrieved from https://www.youtube.com/watch?v=m30ZfJqWq5E

5   Entrepreneur. (2016). The Basics of Branding. Retrieved from https://www.entrepreneur.com/article/280371

6   CEO Hangout. (n.d.). Personal Branding Statistics. Retrieved from https://ceohangout.com/personal-branding-statistics/

7   Istanbul.com. (n.d.). Galata Tower. Retrieved from https://istanbul.com/things-to-do/galata-tower

8   Business Insider. (2012). How to Get One Million Users in Three Weeks: A Case Study. Retrieved from https://www.businessinsider.com/one-million-users-startups-2012-1?op=1

9   YouTube. (2022). Chat GPT to 1MM users [Video file]. Retrieved from https://www.youtube.com/watch?v=JvHJFiNez9E

10   ToolTester. (n.d.). ChatGPT: The Ultimate AI Language Model – Statistics and Facts. Retrieved from https://www.tooltester.com/en/blog/chatgpt-statistics/

11   Kelly, K. (2008). 1,000 True Fans. Retrieved from https://kk.org/thetechnium/1000-true-fans/

12   Krause, A. (2019). An Instagram star with two million followers couldn't sell 36 T-shirts – and it reveals a huge issue with the influencer industry. Retrieved from https://www.insider.com/instagrammer-arii-2-million-followers-cannot-sell-36-t-shirts-2019-5

13   Koetsier, J. (2020). 2 Million Creators Make Six-Figure Incomes On YouTube, Instagram, Twitch Globally. Retrieved from https://www.forbes.com/sites/johnkoetsier/2020/10/05/2-million-creators-make-6-figure-incomes-on-youtube-instagram-twitch-globally/?sh=6422e65723be

14   Nosto. (2019). Consumer Content Report: Influence in the Digital Age. Retrieved from https://www.nosto.com/blog/consumer-content-report-influence-in-the-digital-age/

Chapter 2

15   "Nike Timeline." Wikipedia, The Free Encyclopedia. Wikimedia Foundation, Inc. 21 December 2022. Web. 21 March 2023. https://en.wikipedia.org/wiki/Nike_timeline.

16 "Nike celebrating banned Air Jordans with new release." Yahoo Sports. 15 October 2016. Web. 21 March 2023. https://sports.yahoo.com/news/nike-celebrating-banned-air-jordans-with-new-release-174631314.html

17 "Toyota Prius." Wikipedia, The Free Encyclopedia. Wikimedia Foundation, Inc. 27 September 2022. Web. 21 March 2023. https://en.wikipedia.org/wiki/Toyota_Prius#cite_note-Toyota0909-7

18 "What Percentage of Airline Passengers are Business Class?" Eclipse Aviation. Web. 21 March 2023. https://www.eclipseaviation.com/what-percentage-of-airline-passengers-are-business-class/

19 "The 5 Key Story Elements." Boords. Web. 21 March 2023. https://boords.com/storytelling/the-5-key-story-elements#conflict

20 Chris Vogler, Monolith. - https://blog.reedsy.com/guide/story-structure/heros-journey/

21 Campbell, J. (1949). The Hero with a Thousand Faces. Princeton, NJ: Princeton University Press.

22 The Numbers. (n.d.). The Matrix Movies at the Box Office. Retrieved from https://www.the-numbers.com/movies/franchise/Matrix#tab=summary

Chapter 3

23 Dr Jordan B Peterson, Infamous: When Comedy Exists Outside of Agenda | Andrew Schulz | EP 304, https://www.youtube.com/watch?v=Z6RTYZz4EtQ

24 Gallo, C. (2011, January 18). Steve Jobs and the Power of Vision. Forbes. Retrieved from https://www.forbes.com/sites/carminegallo/2011/01/18/steve-jobs-and-the-power-of-vision/?sh=6f7781ff172b

25 Garcia, Alexia Fernández. "How Airbnb Founders Sold Cereal to Keep Their Dream Alive." Entrepreneur's Handbook, 27 June 2019, entrepreneurshandbook.co/how-airbnb-founders-sold-cereal-to-keep-their-dream-alive-d44223a9bdab

26 Carmody, C. (n.d.). The Numbers Don't Lie: Stories, Not Statistics, Make You Memorable. Speaking CPR. Retrieved from https://speakingcpr.com/the-numbers-dont-lie-stories-not-statistics-make-you-memorable/

27 ltman, G. (2003). How Customers Think: Essential Insights into the Mind of the Market. Boston, MA: Harvard Business Press.

28 Stillman, J. (2018, March 6). How to Write Your Own Personal Mission Statement: 7 Questions to Help You Find Your True North. Inc. Retrieved from https://www.inc.com/jessica-stillman/how-to-write-your-own-personal-mission-statement-7-questions.html

29 Oprah Winfrey's Official Biography. Oprah.com. Retrieved from https://www.oprah.com/pressroom/oprah-winfreys-official-biography/all

30 SmallBizGenius. (2021, April 21). 68 Branding Statistics Every Business Owner Should Know. SmallBizGenius. Retrieved from https://www.smallbizgenius.net/by-the-numbers/branding-statistics/

31   Statista. (2021). Airbnb. Retrieved from https://www.statista.com/topics/2273/airbnb/#dossier-chapter2

32   Lev-Ram, Michal. "Planet Airbnb: Inside Brian Chesky's Plans to Conquer a Reopened World." Fast Company, 13 Apr. 2021, https://www.fastcompany.com/90629637/planet-airbnb-inside-brian-cheskys-plans-to-conquer-a-reopened-world

33   Homa, K. (2011, September 15). "The Internet Is Just A Fad" -- Newsweek, Feb. 26, 1995. Retrieved from https://homafiles.info/2011/09/15/the-internet-is-just-a-fad-newsweek-feb-26-1995/

34   "History of Google". Wikipedia. Retrieved 9 May 2023, from https://en.wikipedia.org/wiki/History_of_Google

35   Ritter, J. (2014, August 7). Google's IPO, 10 Years Later. Forbes. https://www.forbes.com/sites/jayritter/2014/08/07/googles-ipo-10-years-later/?sh=7ac3b4e32e6c

36   Di Lorenzo, Gennaro. "Google Vision Statement & Mission Statement (An Analysis)." FourWeekMBA, 6 Sept. 2019, https://fourweekmba.com/google-vision-statement-mission-statement/

37   Wikipedia contributors. (2022, April 29). Mary Kay Ash. In Wikipedia, The Free Encyclopedia. https://en.wikipedia.org/wiki/Mary_Kay_Ash

38   Mary Kay Inc. "Our Founder." Mary Kay, 2022, https://www.marykay.com/en-us/about-mary-kay/our-founder

39   Entrepreneur. (n.d.). Mary Kay Ash Biography. Retrieved from https://www.entrepreneur.com/growing-a-business/mary-kay-ash-biography/197602

40   Elrod, H. (n.d.). Hal Elrod's Mission. Retrieved from https://halelrod.com/about-hal/elrods-mission/

Chapter 4

41   Koppelaar, R. H. E. M. (2005). Automotive Engines, Theory and Servicing (7th ed.). Clifton Park, NY: Thomson Delmar Learning

Chapter 5

42   CNBC. (2010, June 9). Beachbody's P90X: Making Serious Money. Retrieved from https://www.cnbc.com/2010/06/09/beach-bodys-p90x-making-serious-money.html

43   Moore, T. (n.d.). The Problem Stack. Retrieved from https://www.coachmarketingmachine.com/the-problem-stack/

44   Graham, P. (2006). Life is short. Retrieved from http://paulgraham.com/vb.html

Chapter 6

45   Gladwell, M. (2008). Outliers. New York, NY: Little, Brown and Company

46   Short Fact. (n.d.). How Many Hours a Day Does the Average Person Talk? Retrieved from https://short-fact.com/how-many-hours-a-day-does-the-average-person-talk/

47 Palladio Trusted Advisors AG. (n.d.). Moving Hands Game. Retrieved from https://www.palladio.net/methods/moving-hands-game

48 Mehrabian, A. (1971). Silent Messages: Implicit Communication of Emotions and Attitudes. Belmont, CA: Wadsworth

Chapter 7

49 Ellis, B. (2018, March 5). 4 Simple Ways to Make People Feel Important. RapidStart Leadership. Retrieved from https://www.rapidstartleadership.com/make-people-feel-important/

50 Cherry, K. (2021, February 3). What Is Active Listening? Verywell Mind. Retrieved from https://www.verywellmind.com/what-is-active-listening-3024343

51 Kruse, K. (2021, January 27). The Rule of 7: How Social Media Crushes Old School Marketing [Infographic]. Kruse Control Inc. https://www.krusecontrolinc.com/rule-of-7-how-social-media-crushes-old-school-marketing-2021/

52 Khullar, D. (2018, July 25). Why Do You Forget Names? Time. Retrieved from https://time.com/5348486/why-do-you-forget-names/

53 Kanarek, L. (2021, October 8). How to Actually Remember People's Names. Wired. https://www.wired.com/story/how-to-remember-names/

About the Author

Stephen Steers is a consultant, keynote speaker, storyteller, musician, amateur chef, polyglot and stand-up comedian.

Born to Jamaican parents, raised in Queens, New York, and having lived in six countries, his work across multiple disciplines spans the breadth of the human experience. He is eternally curious about life, skill building and the pursuit of simplicity.

As a consultant and keynote speaker, Stephen has advised more than 700 companies from 28 countries, including teams from Google, Nike, HEC Paris Business School and Entrepreneurs Organization.

Made in the USA
Columbia, SC
08 April 2024

33934900R00145